Wings Over Delft

Praise for *Wings Over Delft*:

'A remarkably engaging story, in which themes of love, art and history are powerfully combined. The unfolding narrative is dramatic, passionate and brilliantly set. The quality of the writing throughout is superb and the ending unforgettably moving.'

Robert Dunbar, critic and broadcaster

'The gentle love story takes the reader through dark intrigue, religious unrest and the palpable, cultural atmosphere of life in a Dutch city, to an unexpected conclusion. A well-tailored and absorbing read for adults as well as for age 12-plus.'
The Sunday Tribune

'Flegg gives us an exquisitely crafted novel which will stay in the reader's memory long after the closing pages are read. The ending is unexpected and dramatic and leaves the reader eagerly awaiting the subsequent books in the Louise trilogy.'

Valerie Coghlan, *Inis*

AUBREY FLEGG was born in Dublin and spent his early childhood on a farm in County Sligo. His later schooldays were spent in England, but he returned to Dublin to study geology. After a period of research in Kenya he joined the Geological Survey of Ireland; he is now retired.

He has published two other books for young people: the first, *Katie's War*, is about the Civil War period in Ireland and won the IBBY Sweden Peter Pan Award 2000. His second book, *The Cinnamon Tree*, is a story of a young African girl who steps on a landmine. Aubrey's books have been translated into German, Swedish, Danish and Serbian.

Wings Over Delft is the first book in the *Louise* trilogy. It will be followed by *The Rainbow Bridge* and *In the Claws of the Eagle*. Aubrey lives in Dublin with his wife, Jennifer; they have two children and two grandchildren.

Wings Over Delft won the Bisto Book of the Year Award 2004, Ireland's most prestigious children's literature prize. It has also been chosen for inclusion in the White Ravens 2004 collection – a selection of outstanding international books for children and young adults made by the International Youth Library in Munich.

Wings Over Delft

Book 1: the Louise *trilogy*

Aubrey Flegg

THE O'BRIEN PRESS
DUBLIN

First published 2003 by The O'Brien Press Ltd,
20 Victoria Road, Dublin 6, Ireland.
Tel: +353 1 4923333; Fax: +353 1 4922777
E-mail: books@obrien.ie
Website: www.obrien.ie
This edition published 2004

ISBN 0-86278-886-2

British Library Cataloguing-in-Publication Data
A catalogue record for this title is available from the British Library

2 3 4 5 6
04 05 06 07 08

Editing, typesetting and design: The O'Brien Press Ltd
Printing: AIT Nørhaven A/S

Author photograph: Jennifer Flegg

The *Louise* trilogy is dedicated
to Bill Darlison

Stop this day and night with me and you shall possess the
  origin of all poems,
You shall possess the good of the earth and sun, (there are
  millions of suns left,)
You shall no longer take things at second or third hand, nor
  look through the eyes of the dead, nor feed on the
  spectres in books,
You shall not look through my eyes either, nor take things
  from me,
You shall listen to all sides and filter them from your self.

  From: 'Song of Myself', Walt Whitman.

Wings Over Delft is dedicated to
my father Bruce Flegg (1900–1984)
who would have heard the beggar sing.

ACKNOWLEDGEMENTS

I have received a lot of help and advice during the writing of *Wings Over Delft*. Firstly, and most importantly, my thanks to my wife, Jennifer, who not only once rescued the manuscript from the wastepaper basket, but has seen it, and me, through its many incarnations. Next are my 'readers': Jan de Fouw, and Margaret and Patrick Kelly, kind friends who read my early draft and shared with me their expert knowledge and critical wisdom. If there are errors of fact they have come from me.

A resounding thanks to all at The O'Brien Press who have been so helpful and encouraging throughout, particularly to Michael O'Brien, Íde ní Laoghaire, and all the production team. I reserve a special thank you, however, for my editor Mary Webb, who has handled both my text and me so sensitively. My gratitude to Children's Book Ireland who, at a critical stage, let me have the use of *The CBI Studio* in the Writers' Centre in Parnell Square, a wonderful resource. Thanks also to all at the Writers' Centre for making me welcome.

Finally my thanks to Bill Darlison, friend, mentor and freethinker to whom the trilogy is dedicated. It was he who issued me with the mental passport to go in search of Louise.

CONTENTS

Mistress Kathenka

Chapter 1
Delft, April 1654

'Annie – please! I don't need a chaperone, not while I am having my portrait painted!' Louise Eeden gazed at her old nurse, torn between love and exasperation. 'I have run wild in this town since I was ten years old, and now you've gone all broody on me.'

The door to master painter Jacob Haitink's house stood open. A diminutive maid had gone to find her mistress. Annie was poking her head inside like a chicken, her nose wrinkling disapprovingly at the lingering smell of stale beer that emerged from the bar that occupied the ground floor below the artist's studio.

'Mistress Kathenka will be here any moment; she can conduct me upstairs. There's no need for you to stay.' Louise thought for a moment, 'Why don't you call in at the Oude Kerk on the way home?' But Annie, like most of the strictly Protestant population of Delft, had her own ideas about 'calling into' a church.

'I'm not a Catholic that I have to use God's house as if it was the baker's or the butcher's.' The old lady shook her head, scattering dark disapproval about her. 'I'll stay here.

Things are … different for you now, Louise. And with your poor mother being ill, I have extra responsibilities …'

'No, Annie! Nothing is different. It's all in your funny old head. Mother is looking so much better these days, and please,' she pleaded, 'don't shake your wattles at me.'

Footsteps sounded on the stairs. Louise put her hand on Annie's arm. 'Here is Mistress Kathenka. I will tell you all about it when I get home.' She took the house-shoes that Annie had been holding for her, slipped off her clogs, arranged them neatly just inside the door, and bent and kissed what she could see of the wrinkled face in the severe bonnet. Then she skipped over to where Mistress Kathenka was standing at the foot of the stairs. She was surprised to find that the Master, who she knew to be an old man, had a wife so young; she could hardly be thirty.

'Louise, isn't it? I'm Kathenka,' the woman introduced herself. Louise began a curtsy, but the other woman just laughed and put an arm around her waist. 'Save that for the Master. Come on up the stairs; they're quite steep.' They mounted steadily. 'Don't worry about your old friend, I'll look after her – your chaperone,' she added.

'Oh don't!' panted Louise.

'Don't look after her?' the mistress queried, puzzled. They had arrived at the second floor landing and paused to get their breath.

'No, it's just the word "chaperone", it implies …' Louise tried a smile, but it faded, and she turned to look down over the Markt. The view through the rough glass was like an oil painting, but an animated one. People, free people, foreshortened to her view, could be seen laying out their stalls below. The silence drew out.

'Implies?' Kathenka asked quietly. It was an invitation, not an intrusion. It caught Louise unaware, she felt a constriction in her throat, and pressed her face against the glass so that her linen head-cloth hid her face.

'It's all my fault,' she whispered. She felt the woman come closer. She stiffened, but there was no touch. 'You see, I've let everybody, even poor Mother, believe that we – Reynier and me – well ... got on. Now, suddenly, it seems that we are engaged.'

'And you're not sure about him ... perhaps there is someone else?'

'No, nobody.' She shook her head against the glass. 'I'm perfectly content in my father's company. We are so close, Father and I. I thought he'd know that Reynier meant nothing to me.' She smiled sadly. 'I thought he'd know instinctively ... absorb it somehow through his skin. But how could he?' She turned and put her back to the window and took a deep breath.

'When we were children, Reynier and I were neighbours. The pottery families stuck together in those days, even if they were at each other's throats in matters of business. First we were toddlers together, then we played together. Then, because having Reynier around meant that other boys left me alone, I was happy to be seen with him. Anyway, we were old friends. He was a way around the problem of elegant young men at the door, clutching their caps and looking for Miss Eeden. There were more interesting things to do than be played court to.'

'And he fell in love with you?'

'Oh no! Look at me!' Louise laughed ruefully. 'Perhaps he thinks he did, but I'm not attractive enough for that. He's handsome; he could have the prettiest girl in town. He's putting a brave face on it. I'm the devil he knows, or thinks he knows. It isn't he who has started the rumours. It is … I don't know … busybodies. You see, I'm a good match.'

What had got her telling all this to a total stranger? Perhaps it was because she reminded her of her mother, years ago, when she had been strong and healthy. Perhaps also it was because the woman was taking it all quite matter of factly.

'And who is this Reynier? What is his surname?'

'DeVries.' Louise heard a small intake of breath, quickly suppressed. 'So, you understand?' she said.

'Oh yes,' Mistress Kathenka nodded. 'The perfect alliance: Eeden's pottery – the best, allied to DeVries's – the largest. What a union! But you don't have to, not if you don't want it!'

'Yes, Mistress, I do. It's my fault, you see. I've never said no to him. I've sheltered behind Reynier all my life. Somehow I've fooled Father, and occasionally even myself, into thinking that Reynier would do. He has been proposing to me since we were children. It came to be a game. I would say, "Not now!" in a jokey sort of way. I just wanted things to stay the same – just Father and me. Now, suddenly, it seems that the town has got tired of waiting and decided for us. Everyone is talking of us as the perfect match. Reynier is as embarrassed about it as I am. He is charming, as always; he says that he wants me, but that I mustn't be forced into it.

He's even taking himself away travelling for a month.'

'And what about the big prize for him: Eeden's pottery?'

'That's another reason for his going away. He says such rumours are disgraceful.' Louise hesitated, then added ruefully. 'He's so honourable it hurts.'

She made to move but the older woman stood in her way. 'And you don't want him?' Louise shook her head dumbly. 'Did you ever say "yes" to this young man?'

'Why no, Mistress, not in so many words …'

'I'm not talking of many words, just one word, child … the word "yes!"'

'I know you are trying to be helpful, Mistress,' Louise said bitterly. 'But you see, the pot is fired now; it can't be turned back into clay. All that remains is to cover it with a pretty glaze – marriage is what they call it.' She lifted her shoulders. 'It is just how things will be. Reynier will get a plain wife, but will inherit Eeden's pottery when Father dies. I will get velvet and silk and …' she smiled wryly, 'a handsome pot for a husband!' She felt her face beginning to crumple. She wanted to throw herself into this woman's arms and cry her heart out, but Mistress Kathenka was having none of that. She held Louise with a level gaze.

'Don't cry, child. It will make your eyes red. I'll take you up to the Master now; he's *my* particular trouble. But if there's not something to be put right here I'm not Kathenka Haitink.' She turned and walked firmly up the stairs ahead of Louise. Louise looked after her.

'Mistress, you won't tell anyone what I have said?' No matter what the Master's wife thought, there was nothing that could be put right; nobody had committed any wrong or sin against her. Yet, as she climbed the creaking stairs, she felt her heart give an involuntary lift.

The mistress was waiting for her at the board door that closed off the top of the stairs; her hand was raised. 'I won't tell anyone, but I think you should. All right?' Louise nodded. The woman looked at her critically, then smiled. 'That's better. And don't stand any nonsense from the Master. He can be as obstinate as a mule, but his heart is in the right place.'

Bad Behaviour

Chapter 2

That morning, before the girl arrived for her portrait, the Master had been behaving abominably.

'She'll be as ugly as sin. You'll see!' he complained over his shoulder as Pieter helped him into his painter's gown. He wiggled his shoulders, then shot his arms out like a scarecrow. The gown had long sleeves, but they were slashed from the wrist to the elbow so that they could hang down out of his way while he painted. 'See this gown, Pieter? Belonged to van Rijn. He gave it to me when we were students together in Leiden.'

'Yes, Master.' If Pieter had heard that story once, he'd heard it a dozen times. He had a strong suspicion that the old scoundrel had stolen the gown from the now famous artist all those years ago.

'Rough painter, van Rijn. Not painterly at all!' Pieter could hear the familiar refrain as he rummaged in the paint cupboard, looking for his master's cap.

'At least his paints don't go solid from lack of use,' he muttered.

'What's that?'

'They say he is very wealthy,' he improvised quickly.

'A man like me shouldn't have to paint for his bread,' the

Master said, sweeping one arm across his chest. 'I should have a patron.'

Pieter smiled to himself, remembering how Mistress Kathenka had called him back as he climbed the stairs to the studio to begin the day's work.

'Psst … here, Pieter. If you let the Master escape from the studio before that girl arrives, you can find somewhere else to work in the evenings.'

Had she seen trouble brewing? Pieter liked Kathenka. She was less than half the Master's age, and mothered and bullied them both by turn. It was she who provided most of the income on which they lived, by running the public house that occupied the ground floor of the premises. As this opened on to the usually crowded Markt, they did well. Pieter often worked for her as a tap-boy of an evening, and was glad of the few stuivers cash.

Now the Master was grumbling again, '… and she won't have a thought in her head. You'll see!' Pieter paid no attention. He spotted the Master's hat on the floor, where he had thrown it down a week ago. He picked it up and started to bang it against his leg. He had his pride, and spiders descending from his master's hat while he was painting would not do.

'What the devil are you doing with that? Give it here.' He snatched it from Pieter's hand. 'Precious hat this.' He walked busily over to the window and pretended to look out, while squinting at his reflection in the glass. He set the floppy white beret at a jaunty angle.

Keeping one eye on his master to make sure he didn't try

to sneak out of the door, Pieter got on with preparing the studio for the sitting. For weeks now he had been working on a new canvas, coating it with size, then lime, and then several layers of gypsum plaster. The final float of plaster of Paris was rubbed so smooth that it looked like ivory. He reached into the back of the cupboard in which they kept their paints, oils and brushes; it was a massive affair, smelling richly of turpentine and linseed oil. He fetched out a shallow box of charcoal twigs and put this down beside the easel. There would be no need for paints today, not at a first sitting. The canvas was just for show.

When he turned around, the Master was still standing at the window, gazing out over the town; he had stopped puffing and blowing for the moment. Pieter knew that view well, having spent many hours looking out, waiting for paint, or size, or plaster to dry. The glass in the leaded panes was rough and uneven. It broke the red roofs across the market square into surprising segments and blobs, so they looked like reflections in water. Low spring sunshine was pouring in from the east, lighting the dust motes that danced in the air about the old man. His white beret was banded with colour from the strip of stained glass that framed the windows. Pieter made a face at his back – the old codger. But when the Master spoke, the petulance was gone from his voice.

'Pieter, you shouldn't be locked up in here with a crotchety old man. You should be chasing young maidens through the meadows beyond the walls.'

What could one do with a man like that? One minute like

a bear on a chain, the next wanting him to chase maidens! It was at times like this, when he surprised him, that Pieter loved the old man. He'd been with him for nearly four years now; apprenticed at fourteen. Soon he would have to move on, work for another master painter, acquire new skills and, if possible, earn enough guilders to pay for membership of the Guild of St Luke. Only then could he teach and sell his pictures as his own. It would be nice to rub shoulders with other members of the Guild as an equal. And as for chasing maidens … Pieter had decided long ago that God had made him with too many angles and bones for the girls to look at him twice, meadows or no meadows.

'Aach!' A thud and an exclamation broke his reverie. 'Ha! Look, Pieter! Didn't I tell you – ugly as sin!' The Master had cracked his head against the glass of the window and was turned towards him, rubbing his forehead and pointing down. It was nonsense; he couldn't see anything properly through those distorting panes.

Suddenly he was pleading. 'Pieter, let's get out of here. Spring calls: you to the meadows, and me to the taproom!' Pieter shook his head. Kathenka might give the Master a wallop on the backside when he acted like this, but something told him that this was more than his master's usual 'old fuss'. He noticed him wiping his hands on his trousers as if they were sweating, and now he produced a groan that could almost be called a whimper. Surely the man couldn't be scared of a mere girl? Then it dawned on him.

'You've been watching her!' he accused. 'You've seen her – and you're scared silly!'

'Of course I've seen her!' snapped his master. 'If you could see beyond the length of your nose I'd make you paint her yourself.' Then he became conspiratorial, 'Tell you what ... we'll scare her off! Watch me.'

'No, you –'

Just then there was a knock on the door. It opened, and Mistress Kathenka came in and stepped to one side.

'Master,' she said, 'Miss Eeden.' She bobbed a curtsy towards him. The girl followed her into the room, looking around to see where the Master was. Then she curtsied too, but deeper, an obeisance almost. Out of the corner of his eye, Pieter was aware of Kathenka, first glaring at the Master and then shooting a warning glance at him. He looked at the girl with interest. Her dress was covered by an unadorned cloak, her face was plain. She had dropped her eyes – demure – he thought. He had seen a dozen rich girls and fine ladies come in that door; this was just another. The Master would do a competent job and get a fat fee for it. There was nothing here for the Master to be agitated about at any rate. The Mistress closed the door and Pieter dropped a chip of lapis lazuli into the hollow of his grinding block. Work had to go on.

Perhaps it was the flash of blue from the precious stone that caught her eye, but the girl looked around. Her glance lasted only a second, for as long as it takes lightning to cross the sky, but in that second Pieter understood what it was that had the Master in a state of agitation. Later he would say that she thrilled and shimmered, as if a sudden light had fallen on blowing silk. At other times he would say that it was as if her whole body had suddenly become transparent – a shell revealing a hidden girl within – someone full of wild wonder, pulsing with life. But by then he was in love with her. At this moment, however, he was realising why the Master had been behaving so strangely.

Two years ago, Jacob Haitink had given Pieter an exercise to do; his challenge was to draw an empty glass, and it nearly killed him.

'Pieter,' the Master had said when at last he had succeeded, 'I have one great fear, and that is that one day someone will walk in that door who is completely without conceit. Someone who is as transparent as your empty glass there. That is a portrait I must never paint, because you see, Pieter, people's conceits are what we paint. We caricature them, we expose their little vanities, we flatter them. But someone who is without conceit is as intangible and as illusive as your empty glass. Truly, if such a person comes in you must stop me, because if I try, it will destroy me.' Pieter looked at the girl again now; the vision had passed. How do you paint something that has no apparent form, no outline, but just exists in numerous reflections and refractions of imagined light? Could this girl really be the Master's nemesis, his end?

Stepping into the studio from the dark stairway, Louise was dazzled by the light. The room was longer and larger than she had expected. It must be a single attic spread over two adjoining houses. The ceiling was arched, following the line of the supporting timbers of the roof. She felt as if she had walked into the inside of an upturned boat. Suffused light from dormer windows on the north side filled the room. The windows to the south were curtained, except for one, through which a blaze of morning sun was streaming. She noticed that the Mistress was curtsying, but couldn't, for the moment, see to whom. Then she saw him, the Master, in the very centre of the stream of sunlight. His pose was dramatic, one arm raised as if to make a proclamation. Her first impression was of a rather squat mediaeval herald in a tabard; all he lacked was a trumpet. When he was sure that she had seen him, he plucked a ridiculous, floppy, white beret from his head, swept it across his chest, and bowed. Louise was delighted and responded with the deepest curtsy she could achieve without actually falling over.

As she rose, she heard Mistress Kathenka close the door behind her. So, she was on her own now, and the Master was hurrying in her direction, swinging his hat across the floor as if sweeping a path for her with it.

'Miss Eeden, you are so welcome!' he boomed, bowing again. 'Come and sit down, you can take your clothes off later; it is still cool … ' Louise blinked – perhaps she did need a chaperone after all? She thought of poor, fussy little Annie below and all her worst fears, but somehow she didn't feel in immediate danger. Out of the corner of her eye she caught a flash of blue, like a glimpse of a kingfisher, skimming fast and low over the water of the Schiekanaal. She turned and found herself staring at a boy, a little older than herself, standing by what looked like a tree stump in the corner of the studio. There was that gleam of blue again! It came from a piece of stone he held in his hand. Of course, an apprentice, the Master would have an assistant. As Louise turned, she caught the boy staring, grim-faced, at his master. But when he saw her looking at him, he smiled, and his smile was big and generous. Her first impression was that he was most wonderfully ugly. He looked as if he had been whittled out of a piece of wood by someone using a blunt penknife. Her heart opened to him in a sudden affinity. She wanted to smile back, but shyness overcame her. Blushing, she turned away, to find the Master busily dusting a chair for her with his hat.

'Sit down, my dear and we will have a little chat.'

As Louise settled herself, she could feel the unaccustomed slip and movement of her dress, as the silk protested beneath her cloak. There were strange and exciting scents. The studio, or this corner of it, had obviously been set up for her portrait. There was an easel with a canvas on it; the wooden stretchers at its back were turned to her. Beyond this was a chair, for the Master, presumably, and a table. She craned to see what was on it: a blue Delft-ware jug containing brushes of various lengths and thicknesses, some green bottles filled with liquids, pottery jars, and what looked like small bladders, all neatly tied at their tops.

'I'll need more white lead, Pieter,' said the Master, fussing with the brushes and poking at the little bladders. He put his floppy hat on, took it off, shook it, and put it back on again. He gave the impression of constant motion. Now he was searching for something.

'Pieter, what have you done with my palette?'

Suddenly, as if remembering his manners, he said, 'Miss Louise, this is my apprentice, Mr Kunst.' The boy with the kingfisher stone bowed. Louise had a smile ready prepared for him this time.

'Well ... ' the Master pursued. 'My palette?'

'It's hanging on the table in its usual place,' the boy replied in a resigned tone. His voice was deep and resonant. 'But, Master, you don't paint on a first day,' he added.

'Of course I do.'

It was difficult for Louise to say at first if the artist was clowning or serious. At the moment he was glaring angrily at his thumb as he tried to fit his palette over it. The thumb emerged and he smiled. 'Now for a brush,' he said, selecting a long slender one from the jug and making a pass with it in the air like a fencer. Louise wasn't sure whether she was supposed to smile or not. His moods seemed to change like quicksilver. Without warning, he turned to her, and spread his arms wide as if pleading.

'Miss Eeden, surely you don't want to be cooped up in here with a mad old painter and his imbecile apprentice! Look, the sun is splitting the skies.' He made a vague gesture with his palette. 'Wouldn't you prefer to be out there? Come back some other day when – ' A sharp cough from the boy in the corner cut him short; the Master turned and glared at the him and then snapped: 'Get on with your work.'

'Oh no, I *want* to be here,' Louise assured him. 'I really do. This is far more interesting.' Her answer appeared to surprise the painter, and his eyebrows shot up, nearly disappearing under his hat.

'Oh indeed? *Interesting*. Do you hear that, Pieter?' he said, turning to where the boy was working, jutting a defiant chin at him. 'And there was you wanting a day off so you could go chasing young maidens through the meadows. Here is a lesson for you, a young lady who is actually *interested* in our work!'

Louise felt a blush mounting. She hadn't meant to get the boy into trouble. But the Master was smiling now, as if he had settled a small score. He pretended to flex the paintbrush in his hand like a rapier. Then, in another sudden change of mood, he put down his palette, dropped the brush into the jug, and turned to her. She noticed that his smile crinkled his eyes into a thousand bright lines.

'So, I am to paint a portrait of Miss Louise Eeden?'

'Yes, Master, please. That is my father's wish.'

'But it is not yours?'

'Oh yes, it is,' she said.

He bowed in acceptance. Louise was relieved that he was being serious; it made it easier. She had rehearsed this bit, because she had her own ideas of how she wanted her portrait painted. 'Master,' she said, 'I am familiar with your pictures. That is why I wanted to come to you. I am no grand lady, nor do I have the looks to … to be admired. I just want to be painted as I am.'

'But, my dear, that is what a portrait is.'

She felt panicky now; it was difficult to explain. She knew what everyone expected – it was part of the conspiracy – the portrait of an heiress on the eve of her marriage. She couldn't tolerate that, but how could she say this without giving offence?

'Of course, Master, but, how can I put it ... I don't want to be painted like a grand lady – looking as if I had a lemon in my mouth.' His eyebrows were rising again, so she hurried on. 'You remember your portrait of the Beggar at the Begijnhof gate? That old man, I love him, he lives. I want to live in my portrait, too. Let me be painted playing my lute, or looking through the telescope Father and I are building. Nobody wants to look at Miss Louise Eeden sitting stiff as a stuffed parrot. Let me just be "Girl in a green dress".' Louise was running out of words. He *had* to understand. But he was laughing at her.

'No, no, no, my child. That's not a portrait you are talking about; it is a tronie. It's the sort of picture we paint when funds are low. Pieter and I painted that picture of the beggar together, didn't we? What did we pay him, Pieter? A few stuivers to sit for us in the studio here, and then we hunted his fleas for a fortnight. The people who buy tronies want the beggar without the fleas. Your father is the finest potter in Delft,' he bowed, 'a member of the Guild of St Luke. He would never accept a mere tronie of his daughter. There is custom and practice in these things. We all know why a father wants his daughter painted at a time like this. This is a moment to stop the world, to show it that he has brought up a girl of beauty and fashion. Can you imagine him accepting a picture showing, "Miss Eeden dressed as a bargee's daughter on the occasion of her engagement to –"'

'No!' Louise shouted, surprised at herself. 'On the occasion of nothing!' She half rose, taking breath. She had to kill this off once and for all. But a change had taken place in the Master; he was leaning forward, one hand held out as if to stop her. The paintbrush, which he had been holding, went skittering across the floor. She wondered if he was ill, having a seizure? But he was whispering at her, a hoarse, urgent sound.

'Stop! Don't move!' She realised that he was trying to prevent her getting up. She deflected her protest by swivelling away from him. She looked up and found herself staring straight into the eyes of the boy with the blue stone. For what seemed like an eternity, none of them moved.

Tap tap ... tap tap. Tap tap ... a pigeon had landed on the windowsill and was pecking at the glass. The sound broke the spell. The bird cocked its head sideways and peered into the studio expectantly. The Master sighed.

'Pieter, feed our friend, will you.' Louise watched the boy cross to the window, open it and shake some grain on to the windowsill. There was a soft *froo froo* and the hollow peck of a beak on the wood. Louise stared at the bird, her thoughts confused. What had she said? You don't argue with a master of his trade. You don't tell him how to do his job. He was coming towards her now, a polite handshake and it would be over. To her surprise she felt his fingers, gentle on her cheek, and he turned her face towards him.

'Come, my love. I will paint you as you wish.'

'Like the beggar at the Begijnhof gate?'

'So that you live, my heart, and will live as long as paint

and canvas last.' She looked up into the old man's face, a creased conflict of lines. 'It will hurt us both, you know. You don't become a beggar from sleeping in a feather bed.'

'And you, Master?' She asked, worried at the pain in those deep-etched lines. He smiled, but as he turned away she caught the words: 'Me? … me it could destroy.'

He bent to pick up the brush he had dropped. 'In a moment, Miss Louise Eeden,' he said as he straightened up, 'we will begin again. I have seen the beggar in you, but I will have to wake him. Listen to me now, because we have just one chance to find him. If I call out for you to hold your pose again you are to do so, and you will not move an inch nor twitch a muscle. If you move once it will be over and I will paint you with eleven lemons in your mouth and marry you off to Pieter here!' He flexed his brush and made a pass at the boy; the clown had returned.

Galileo

Chapter 3

'So, I am to paint Miss Louise Eeden as we painted the beggar at the Begijnhof gate,' the Master said, gazing up at the ceiling. 'It makes me itch just to think of him. But how about your father? If his daughter refuses to sit for me as the young lady he might expect, will he approve of her as a beggar, and more importantly, will he pay?'

'Oh he will pay, and I'm *sure* he never meant it to be a formal portrait. I think he only thought about a picture of me when he bought the silk for my dress.'

'Ah! The famous silk dress. Come, let us see it. Your father told me, and I'm afraid my heart sank.' He came over to her. 'Your cloak … if I may help?' Louise stood up. She loosened the clasp and he lifted the cloak from her shoulders and stepped back. The captive silk cascaded around her with a whisper.

'Aah!' The Master sighed, and the sound of grinding stopped. He walked around her, breathing heavily through his nose. 'Green silk from China … silk of Cathay! Bought from the very ship, your father says. Do you see it, Pieter? A challenge, eh! Your father did not exaggerate. But do you know how difficult it is for us to paint in green? There is no such thing as a green paint to match this, no green that we can pound up and smear on our palette. The colours in this dress will have to be built up layer upon layer. Pieter, bring over a piece of the lapis lazuli you are grinding.' He waited while the boy came across the room and opened his hand. There it was – the brilliant blue she had seen that moment when she had come into the room.

'Beautiful,' she whispered.

'Don't you ask why we use blue and not green?' the Master queried.

'You have already said, Master, that there is no green paint you can use, so that means you must use blue and yellow. But to grind up jewels is beyond belief, and how do you mix them? The yellow that you use must be clear and translucent for the blue to shine through.'

'Listen to her, Pieter.' Master Haitink said with unfeigned surprise. 'The young lady knows more about our business than is safe. Perhaps she is a spy sent by that rogue Fabritius to learn our secrets. We must take care.'

'You forget, Master,' reminded his apprentice, 'that you have not told even me how you compound your yellows. It is your last secret.' The boy tossed the blue stone in the air and walked back to his corner.

'Last secret indeed! The day you get your indentures back, Pieter, I will tell you.' He stepped back, looking at Louise in admiration. 'Oh, Miss Eeden let me paint you standing there. I will put a crown on your head and a sceptre in your hand.'

'And all eleven lemons in my mouth?' laughed the girl.

'Sit, child. Let me prepare you; I have a vision to capture again.' Louise sat, while his hands flew over her, detached and professional, arranging the folds of the dress, fluffing out the white linen sleeves of her blouse where they emerged from the stiff, half-sleeved bodice. 'So this is the latest fashion?' he said, as he lifted the white linen cloth from her head and explored where Annie had rolled her hair at the back. She had bound the roll of hair with a double strand of seed pearls. 'With your permission ... ' he undid one of the strands so that it could hang free. 'Now, see, it frames your face.' He stood back then and frowned.

'Pieter,' he said. 'We have too much light in here.' He tapped his foot impatiently while the boy crossed the room and drew the curtains against the morning sun. The stream of yellow light was snipped off and the room darkened. The boy joined his master, and they both stood staring at the dress.

'Surely you want all the light you can get?' asked Louise, disappointed and uncomfortable under their joint scrutiny.

'Oh no, it is not quantity, but quality of light that we need. Look down at your dress, to where I am pointing, and you will understand what I mean. Tell me, what colours do you see?'

Louise looked and was puzzled. 'Colours ... ? Well, green ... ?'

'Ah yes, green, but what green? How many greens? Look, here within the folds.' He pointed to a deep fold that opened from her right knee. 'See ... down in here, where the light is less, the green is darker. Now we rise towards

30

the light.' As Louise followed his finger, it was as if she was watching a magic brush trailing a continuum of different shades of green behind it.

'Yes, Master, I see!' she said delightedly. 'Why did I never notice? There are thousands of greens here.'

'Ah ha! People just don't *see*. And look, where the light from the crest of this fold is reflected into the almost black shadow of the fold next to it? Here we have reflected light. That is why Pieter closed the curtains. Now, with light coming just from the windows facing north, no one colour dominates. Each colour, while subdued, is correct in relation to the colours around it.'

'Father says that all the colours in the world are hidden in a single beam of light. That a rainbow isn't painted onto the sky but is made from the way light shines on the rain.' She was beginning to enjoy herself. Men – other than Father, that is – never talked to her like this. She wanted to ask him about the other colours, but then she realised that he had backed away from her. She looked up; he was observing her with his head cocked to one side. The look went on and on. Then he said, almost to himself:

'I see you, child. You are like a sneeze that will not come.' In a normal voice he said: 'Tell me about your father. There are some in town that are suspicious of people who delve into mysteries like the nature of light. Some people believe that we should leave the heavens to God and let him paint the rainbows in the sky. Your father is a freethinker?'

Louise nodded enthusiastically. 'Father says we must

question everything. He plans to introduce philosophy in the school if he is elected to the Town Council.'

'Does he, indeed?' The Master was looking at her again; his eyes were narrowed this time. He picked up a slender paintbrush and idly fingered the bristles as if they made the point of a sword. 'You say he is building a telescope?'

'We *both* are!' Louise corrected, but added, a little lamely, 'Well, actually the cooper from the pottery is making the tube for us.'

'Your honesty is commendable, my dear, but that will not protect you from error.' He dropped the brush back into its jug and squared up to her, hands on hips. 'I suppose you support this newfangled idea that the earth spins about the sun?'

Louise was taken aback. Did anyone still believe that the earth stood stationary, and that the sun moved around it? She glanced across at the apprentice; he half-smiled and dropped his gaze. The Master, who had seen her look, growled. 'Get on with your work, Pieter, you won't understand our learned discussion here.' She felt indignant for the young man; there was nothing she could do for him, but she could challenge the Master.

'Can it really be, sir, that you think that the sun spins about the earth?' she asked.

'Of course it does. Use the evidence of your eyes. The sun rises in the east – or it did when I last looked – it traverses the heavens, and then it sinks in the west. It doesn't achieve this by standing still, my dear.'

'But, Galileo –'

'Galileo be damned,' he interrupted rudely. 'If the sun did not move, then the earth would have to spin like a top to compensate. You, my dear, would be thrown off it, so too would every movable object. Pigs would fly; even Pieter would be snatched from his just deserts at the gates of hell. Look what happens!' To Louise's alarm, the artist began to spin. 'Watch my sleeves,' he shouted as he flashed around. 'See how they fly out! You, my dear, would be spun off the globe and would crack your head on the floor of heaven before you could say lapis lazuli.' Here he lost balance and collapsed onto the low chair behind his easel where Louise could only see his legs. 'Give up, my dear. You may not have heard of Aristotle, the Greek philosopher, but he got it right; we have no authority to change our minds … ' Then he groaned, 'Lord how the room swims.'

Louise smiled. Serve you right, she thought, but she was relieved that he hadn't done himself an injury. Nevertheless, she resented his presumption that she had not heard of Aristotle.

'You mean Aristotle's crystalline spheres, I presume?' she said, and cocked her head, waiting for his response. Slowly his head appeared around the edge of the canvas. 'Pieter,' he said humbly. 'Miss Eeden knows her Aristotle. We must look to our laurels.'

'Eight spheres,' Louise said, conscious that she was showing off. The Master rose carefully, holding on to the edge of the canvas to steady himself. He began to incant, his voice taking on a dreamy, inward sounding tone.

'At the centre lies the earth, changeable and corruptible;

about this circles the moon, a celestial orb, perfect and incorruptible. This is the divine plan. Then come the eight crystalline spheres slipping past each other, each with its own heavenly burden: one for the sun, and seven for the planets. Then comes the outer firmament, in which are embedded the fixed stars, the stars that do not change.' As the Master spoke he used his hands, eloquently describing the spheres for Louise in the air in front of him. She was moved, and a little ashamed at having shown off. It was indeed a beautiful concept, and it had a divine simplicity, but she had to respond.

'Master, I would like to think that you were right, but with our telescope we will see things that I'm afraid prove beyond doubt that these beautiful crystal spheres cannot in fact exist. How will you explain the movements of the four moons that circle Jupiter? How can these circle the planet if Jupiter is set in crystal – frozen as if in ice?'

'The answer, my dear, is simple; they cannot, therefore there is no point in looking!'

'But –'

He held up his hand. 'No *but*, my dear. You have described it perfectly. If you look through the clear ice of a canal in winter you will often see a fish that has become frozen into it. If I were to tell you that smaller fishes could be seen swimming through the ice about it, you would dismiss me for a fool because fish can't swim in ice, no more can moons orbit in crystal. It is therefore a waste of God's time to look.'

Louise was dumbfounded. She shook her head; he

really meant what he had said! Speaking as clearly and precisely as she could, she said: 'On the contrary, Master, I would look and, if they did move, I would tell you that you were mistaken. That the fish could not be frozen in the ice as you thought, just as I tell you now, Jupiter cannot be set in crystal.'

'But, child, what arrogance! Don't you know in your heart that supreme concepts are greater than mere facts? That the sacred Aristotle's model of the universe must outweigh the observations of a sixteen-year-old girl with a telescope? Your telescope lies.' Louise's head was beginning to swim. She wasn't sure whether to laugh or to cry. What made it worse was the realisation that she liked this cantankerous old man. She wanted his approval more than anything, but he belonged in the past. What could she do? She felt the blood surging into her face, a sure sign of danger. When she flared like this with Annie she usually said something that she regretted. But truth would out.

'Sir, how can a telescope lie?' she demanded. 'When we get our lenses I will show you, and you will see with your own eyes.' She looked up at him. She was pleading, but it was no use; he had clapped his hands over his eyes.

'No, I will not look. There is no need. It is not for me to change; it is your belief in your instrument that is at fault.'

Louise had had enough. She gathered herself for a final thrust, then she would go. 'If Aristotle had had a telescope, Master,' she said, 'he would have looked, but unlike you, he would have changed his mind. Respectfully sir, you are two thousand years out of date.' She leant forward, preparing to rise and leave this place. She was bitterly disappointed. She had won the argument, but at what price? She even felt the victor's burst of compassion for the vanquished. It was then that she looked up.

Everything in the studio seemed to have changed. The apprentice was bent towards her, gripping the sides of his grinding block. The Master had his hands held out to stop her, freezing her in her place. In one all-encompassing instant Louise Eeden realised that the victory was not hers, but his. She had fallen into a trap. She could hear him shouting as he scrabbled for a stick of charcoal. His voice seemed to come from a distance.

'Nay, nay child, don't move!' But he had opened her like an oyster, she had no wish or mind to move. She froze for him, and she held that pose, it seemed forever.

Pieter hadn't been listening, his mind had wandered; their argument meant little to him. For a while he had tried to see in the girl the look that had so intrigued him when she came in, but it was gone. He concentrated on scrutinising each chip of lapis for traces of the grey limestone from which it had been chipped. The smallest trace would cause the paint to sicken and fade. He began the cautious business of grinding. Then suddenly he heard the Master shouting, and looked up, startled.

'Ja, ja, ja, the old man has gone too far this time. I see it on your face. You reproach me. You are angry, but inside you are smiling at the old fool. God forgive me!' the old man declared. 'But now, for the first time child, you look beautiful. Aach, it hurts!' His hand had found a piece of charcoal, but it was shaking so much that Pieter wondered if he would ever be able to draw with it. 'Even if it turns you into stone, don't move, don't change.' He took the trailing end of his painter's sleeve and hurriedly wiped his eyes. 'Mijn Gott, look, you have me weeping ... '

Pieter was staring at the girl, open-mouthed. 'Pieter!' he yelled without turning. 'You have stopped grinding. I must hear you! Nothing must change.' The boy glanced at the blue powder in the hollow of the grinding block. Ultramarine, their most expensive pigment, and soon it would be too fine. If it got too fine the colour would deaden and he would be in trouble. He dropped some more chips of precious lapis into the hollow and recommenced grinding. The stone moved rhythmically, *Crish ... crish...* but he, like the Master, was in the grip of the moment. Some magic, emanating from that girl, possessed them both. He forgot about the world, the studio, and even the summer sun outside. *Crish ... crish*, and the sound of his grinding became wing-beats of the angel that seemed to hover over their heads. The carillon on the Nieuwe Kerk chimed, and then chimed again. Still she held her pose. His eyes moved back and forth: to the girl – Miss Louise Eeden – the name didn't mean anything to him then, and then to the Master, hunched over his sketchbook, working ... failing ... turning the page ... working.

Pieter examined her pose. She was leaning slightly forward. Yes! The Master was right; she had been about to get up, to walk out and leave at the moment when he called on her not to move. Her body was like a spring ready to be released. But it was when Pieter looked at her face that he felt a stab of that pain that had caused the Master to cry out. Yes, there was reproach there, but behind that there was something more, laughter perhaps, something that made him long to be the subject of that look, to pass the barrier and be accepted. Love was too sweet a word and compassion was too grand. His grinding faltered as strange emotions filled his mind, but then Pieter thought of the Master, pinned like a moth under her gaze, and realised that the old man was out there on his own. Pieter was his apprentice and they both needed the soothing sound of his grinding stone.

Slowly the intensity of the vision faded – he could not have borne it if it had gone on much longer – and the face of the young girl re-emerged. He reckoned she would be sixteen years of age, about two years his junior. At last the Master was working steadily. He had thrown down his sketching book and was drawing directly on to the canvas with bold, deft lines. Pieter's stone circled in the now ruined blue and her name repeated itself again and again in his mind: 'Louise … Louise … '. He wasted more than three guilder's worth of lapis by over-grinding that morning, though the Master never reproved him.

Time passed, but still the Master continued to draw. Pieter knew that the painter was exhausted, but he guessed too that he didn't know how to stop. He began to laugh. The girl looked up at him. He raised an eyebrow at her, a smile flickered across her face. The magic faded; the sitting was over.

Louise straightened painfully. She had held the pose for an hour or more and every muscle protested at the unnatural strain. As she relaxed, Pieter saw her put her hand over her mouth to hide the look that she had preserved so long for the Master. It was a childlike gesture that tore at Pieter as he hurried to help the Master rise. Louise noticed that the old man was in difficulties and she reached out to lend a hand. Together they pulled the Master to his feet. Then they held hands in a circle, smiling at each other, like dancers in a set, holding on to that special moment before the music starts again. The Master was the first to break away, shuffling and growling as he padded off towards the window, scrubbing at his face with his hat.

'Pieter!' he said. 'Escort Miss Eeden home.' Pieter looked at her, but she was watching the old man as he hunched against the light, and smiling to herself.

Chapter 4

Pieter helped Louise on with her cloak, handed her the linen head-cloth, and opened the door for her. But when he gestured for her to precede him down the stairs, she hesitated, and then asked him to go ahead.

'You can catch me if I fall,' she said, but he noticed her stop and look anxiously out of the landing window on the way down. Then, when they reached the bottom of the stairs, she touched his arm. 'Mr Kunst, there is someone I … wish to avoid. She may be here still. Could you look for me?' Pieter sauntered into the taproom and looked around. There was nobody there, but in the partitioned-off snug he could see Kathenka talking to an elderly woman. He wandered back and said in a low voice.

'Yes, there is an old woman … brown dress, apron, severe-looking coif? She has her back to us. She's talking to the Mistress.'

'Thank you,' the girl smiled. 'Come on, quickly!' She slipped past Pieter, ran lightly to the open door, picked up her clogs, and stepped outside with them. Pieter looked towards Kathenka as he followed. To his surprise she winked at him.

'We will go this way,' the girl said, turning away from the

Town Hall towards the Nieuwe Kerk. The Markt was busy now. Stalls had been set up and she threaded her way through the throng. It was bright and busy after the shade and quiet of the studio. Pieter followed, feeling shy and ill-at-ease. He realised that his presence had been imposed on her and that she might not want to be seen with him as a consort. He was not good in a crowd. God had blessed him with too many bones and, in company, they just seemed get everywhere. His confidence tended to desert him once he left the studio. In school they had called him 'Pieter the Puppet', the little ones imitating his walk to a T. The trouble was that this was just how he felt: as if he was hung on strings manipulated by a not very competent puppeteer.

One day, when Pieter had made a mistake in spelling the word 'horse', the teacher had called him up and told him to draw a horse on the blackboard. It was meant as a punishment. Snorts and titters followed him as he ricocheted off the desks on the way to the board. Then his fingers touched the chalk and a change came over him; for once he no longer feared what his body might do. He just knew that the horse of his dreams was waiting for him inside that board. He reached high; the chalk swept across the black surface, and there was the horse, springing out at him in that one streaming line. Five more lines and an almond eye, to reveal the rest of the horse to the class, and he was walking back to his desk. They didn't laugh at him for a whole day. That night his mother had said that St Luke, patron saint of artists, had held his hand, but that he was never to mention it. They were Catholics, and Catholics were barely tolerated in the town of Delft.

Pieter was woken from his daydream by nearly colliding with the girl as she halted in front of him. He stopped in a flap of arms and legs. A young man, smartly dressed in the clothes of a gentleman apprentice, had stepped gracefully into her path. He was bowing to her and holding her hand. He heard the young mistress exclaim, 'But I thought you had departed!'

Pieter backed away so as not to eavesdrop on their conversation. He recognised the young man. They had been at school together. Reynier was his name and he was everything that Pieter was not. For a start he was wealthy and was heir to the largest of the town's many potteries, but the chief difference was that he was gloriously assured and at ease with himself, as well as being outwardly charming and personable. Pieter retreated further. They looked well together, the young man of fashion and the poised girl with her modish head-cloth, but Pieter had private reasons to be disturbed.

All at once there was a break in the apparent harmony ahead; he heard the girl's voice rise.

'... Mr Kunst is seeing me home, thank you, Reynier.' She turned. 'Mr Kunst, have you met Reynier DeVries?' Pieter stepped forward and jerked his hand out. For a brief second Reynier seemed put out, but his manners reasserted themselves.

'Of course I have!' he said pleasantly. 'How do you do, Pieter.' He shook Pieter's hand as if it were loose. 'We were at school together,' he told the girl. 'Pieter drew a wonderful horse.' It was gallantly said, but Pieter wondered why it was that his beautiful horse suddenly seemed mean and insignificant now.

'Yes, I have seen Mr Kunst's work!' the girl said pointedly. 'Now, we should be getting on. I wish you the very best for your journey.' The young man stepped back, bowing, but still holding her hand. Then he drew her towards him. It was a graceful movement, a kiss on the cheek? It looked like an accident, but at that moment the girl turned her head and the man's lips met her head-cloth instead. Pieter saw a flash of anger cross Reynier DeVries's face before it was replaced by an easy laugh.

'Goodbye Pieter!' he said. 'Don't get your strings crossed.'

Pieter opened his mouth to say something, but a forgotten stammer tangled his tongue. His hands gestured vaguely, and Reynier was gone.

Pieter stood rooted, deep in thought. He saw Louise start off towards the Nieuwe Kerk. Could this be her intended? Reynier DeVries, who, despite all his easy charm, had made his school days a misery? It was Reynier who had first called him 'The Puppet'and who had then gone out of his way to chide the younger boys who took up the name. 'Now, now, come on lads, that's not fair,' he would say, putting his arm protectively over Pieter's shoulder. The gesture seemed to say: I'm Pieter's particular friend … Pieter's protector. But, damn him, Pieter's tormentor, too. For brief periods Pieter had loved Reynier with the all-forgiving love of a boy for a hero. But Reynier always found some subtle way to put him down.

Pieter broke out of his reverie. He clenched his fists.

'He's a bully… a bully!' he said out loud, and a woman, pre-
siding over a stall of spring onions, looked at him and
shrieked:

'Saying your prayers, Mr Kunst?'

Then, laughing uproariously at her own joke, she turned
to repeat it to the woman on the next stall. Pieter, who
hadn't even realised he had said anything, looked at her in
astonishment, then he hurried off after the vanishing girl.

Louise had felt the brush of Reynier's attempted kiss as she
turned from him in the Markt. If she had seen it coming she
mightn't have had the courage to fend him off, but now that
she had, she felt a brief glow of satisfaction. She wove in
and out of the market stalls, her long cloak and rustling silk
incongruous on this sunny spring day. The heat and the
constriction began to oppress her. She was thinking about
Reynier. She hadn't expected to see him. He had said a
formal goodbye when he had told her of his intention to
travel, ostensibly to help quench the rumours that had
started about their engagement. If he wanted to quench
rumours, kissing her in the Markt was not the way to do it.
Ever since they were little, he'd been protective of her. He
was two years older than she was, but he had always been
prepared to play her games. When they were little, they had
played at being married. Then, when she was old enough
to feel uneasy, she'd got out of the game by making it a joke
between them. There had been times when she had
thought that she was in love with him, but it was a feeling

that never lasted long; there were always more interesting things to do.

She thought back to their last meeting, a week ago, when she first learned that there were rumours abroad. She had been at home. She heard a knock at the door but had ignored it. The C string on her lute had just snapped and was wrapped around her left wrist. It was her fault, she hadn't played in a while and had tuned up too quickly. Voices came through from the hall as she was rummaging in her workbasket where she kept her spare strings. She found one, knotted the end, and levered out the tiny ivory peg that would hold it in the bar at the bottom of the lute. Next she turned her attention to unwinding the broken string from the tuning peg at the neck. She was totally absorbed in this endeavour when a man's hand, encircled by a lace cuff, reached down and lifted the lute from her lap. It was Reynier.

'Allow me,' he said, with a smile. For a moment she was irritated; she liked to do things for herself. But Reynier had long claimed the right to rescue her whether she needed it or not.

'I didn't hear you come in,' she said.

'I was speaking to Annie in the hall, asking after your poor mother; I hear she has had a bit of a relapse.' Louise was about to say something about her mother's cough, but he swept on. 'Annie is an ally of mine in the pursuit of Louise.' This was the old game. Louise grimaced and watched as he made heavy work of unwinding the string. He soon got tired of it and put the lute down. 'What's this rumour I hear?' he asked.

'Rumour?' Louise was indifferent to rumours; she wanted to get on with stringing her lute.

'They are saying in town that Eeden's and DeVries's potteries may come together.'

'Oh? I hadn't heard. But then we are away from things here in the new house.' Louise was surprised at the news. Her father had rather a poor opinion of the pots produced by DeVries, although she couldn't very well say that. 'It will just be a rumour,' she said, indifferently, and reached out for her lute. But Reynier moved quickly and caught hold of her wrist.

'Louise,' he said reproachfully. 'You are not thinking of your father.' He loosened his grip and started caressing her hand.

'Of course I think about Father.' Louise's face burned, what had she got wrong now? Reynier had a way of wrongfooting her. She wanted to withdraw her hand, but his grip, though loose, held her. What if she tried to pull back and he would not let go? It would precipitate something, she wasn't sure what. He was speaking to her as if she were a child.

'Just think, Louise, how it would be if the potteries joined. Your father is the finest painter of Chinaware in Delft. Humble old DeVries would continue to churn out tiles and cups and tableware, and he would be free to do the great vases and pieces of which he is the Master.'

So that was what it was about. Eeden's pots were indeed the most beautiful in Delft, but the money came from the humbler tableware. The more cups and tiles they made, the less time poor Father had to do the really delicate work for which he was justly famed. If the potteries joined, then DeVries's could take over the routine work, and Father could concentrate on the decorative work he loved and which would bring honour and distinction to the venture. She was repentant now.

'Do you think that it is possible? I … I just didn't think …' Reynier raised her hand to his lips and kissed it.

'Of course you didn't, why would you?' he said, releasing her hand. Louise was so tired of being in the wrong; Reynier was really a better person than she.

'Do *you* believe that they can come to some arrangement? Father hasn't mentioned it.' Rather than answering straight away, Reynier turned and walked over to the window. His hair was long and swept down over the broad linen collar that spread out on to his cloak. When he replied he seemed to be measuring his words.

'Louise … there is another rumour going around.' He paused. She had started to reach for her lute again but stopped, gazing at his back. 'I deplore it,' he continued, 'but yet again I wish it were true.'

A prickle of apprehension chased up the backs of Louise's arms. Then Reynier turned and was striding towards her. He appeared to be about to kneel, but instead he clapped one fist into the palm of the other. 'Louise,' he said. 'They are saying that … that this deal is contingent on our getting married.' Louise looked up at him, thunderstruck. Her mouth opened in amazement. She wasn't going to speak, but Reynier stopped her nonetheless. 'No, no! Louise. You mustn't say. I know your answer, and even if by some

miracle you said yes, I could not accept it as your true incli-
nation. I will go away, it is time that I travelled.' He waved
an arm vaguely … 'England, France?' he paused, 'Italy perhaps. Father can spare me. That is why I have come here today: to say goodbye. We must let this blow over; then I may
come to you truly on my knees. It will be six months before I
see you again. Oh Louise, how I will miss you'. He took her
hand and pressed it to his lips, while she, out of sheer bewil-
derment, failed to snatch it away. 'Don't forget your father,
Louise …' He hit his chest as if in determination. 'But I stand
back! I must leave now.' Then, with a swirl of his cloak, he
turned and strode to the door so quickly that Louise's memory was, not of him, but of Annie in startled retreat, as he
swept past her and out into the street.

That had been a week ago. Louise had heard no more.
She had presumed that he had left. It was then that she realised that the world was beginning to change about her. It
started with Annie fussing over how Louise dressed, and
scolding her for going out on her own. Then Father, all
gruff and affectionate, came back from Amsterdam with the
green silk for her dress. There were comments at home
about the merging of the two potteries, but then the subject
was dropped. Mother – pale and translucent in her illness –
went about the house touching things, with a secret smile
that Louise couldn't fathom. The changes were subtle, more
that unrelated things were beginning to orbit around her,
instead of her orbiting around them. It was as if she had become a small sun, the centre of some invisible focus.
Gradually it dawned on her that there really were rumours

about Reynier and her. But how these had come about, and who had spread them, she had no idea. Annie?, she asked herself. No, Annie was just a willing conspirator. Reynier, then? But Reynier was doing the honourable thing and going away specifically to dispel these rumours. She kept thinking about Father, and what it would mean to him to be free to do the work he loved, his business responsibilities shared. She thought of all those childhood games with Reynier, so innocent. Then, more recently, of his ardent proposals and her ambiguous replies. For all that he was gallant, she was sure Reynier did not love her; he could have the pick of the girls in town. Had she unintentionally woven a web, with her accessibility and – let's face it – her fortune, and trapped the young man? The DeVries family were well off, but Reynier had always had an appetite for more.

The Markt was hot and crowded. It was as if the sticky threads of the web were clutching at her, dragging at her heavy clothes. She wanted to scream. Her feet came up against something soft and yielding, and this time she did shriek. Feathery clusters of mute, wide-eyed chickens lay across her path, their legs tied together. She turned and gathered herself, walking faster and faster. She had to get out of the crowded Markt to where she could breathe fresh air and see sky. She skirted a loaded trestle piled with cabbages, only to come up against a flat handcart shouldering a pyramid of smooth waxed cheeses, round as cannon balls. She wanted to tip the table over and send the cheeses bowling through the market place. No one would want her then!

Louise reached the deep shade along the side of the Nieuwe Kerk and stood there, panting. There were footsteps behind her. Why couldn't she be left alone – surely it wasn't Reynier following her? She swung around. It was Mr Kunst, the apprentice; she'd forgotten all about him. He had been told to escort her home. But she didn't want to go home. She decided she'd walk on, perhaps he would turn back. They emerged at the back of the Nieuwe Kerk, Mr Kunst still following discreetly. They crossed a small arched bridge over one of the numerous canals that formed a grid of water throughout the town, and turned left. He would see that she was on her way home now – the Vrouwenregt led towards the Doelen where she lived. But the long, uneven strides continued behind her. When she turned right, away from the Doelen towards the town walls, the boy followed. She didn't want him near her. She felt corrupted. Reynier's attempt at that very public kiss still burned on the side of her face. She rubbed at it, then whipped around in anger. She watched as the boy stumbled awkwardly to a halt, his arms swinging loosely from his shoulders. The tart comment she had planned faded on her lips. What was there about that walk and the way his arms moved? It conjured up an image that she couldn't quite identify. Reynier had said something to him, something about strings. Suddenly she understood: a puppet, of course. That's what Reynier was alluding to. Righteous anger boiled inside her. How dare Reynier make fun of this boy.

'Mr Kunst … ' she demanded, glaring at him. 'May I call you Pieter?' He seemed taken aback.

'Of course, mistress …'

'No!' she corrected impatiently. 'Louise, please … just Louise.' Her anger was bursting out in all the wrong places. 'And look …' she indicated the distance between them. 'We're not strangers. Come, I need you.' She turned and looked into the canal that ran down the middle of the road, a perfect mirror to the houses opposite. He arrived at her side. 'Pieter,' she said without looking up from the water. 'That was my old nurse that I dodged when we left the Master's house. I don't want to deceive you, but she chatters, and I need time to think. Would you be kind enough to take me to the town walls? Your master will not object, will he?'

'No,' he said with a smile. 'He will not miss me, and I promise not to chatter.'

'May I take your arm?' A bony elbow was held out to her and they walked on in silence. A few houses down, their path was blocked by a group of men preparing to haul a finely carved linen chest up to a top floor window. White-painted beams stuck out from the gable-ends of all the houses on the road, and they had attached a pulley to one of these. The chest would be swung through the big up-stairs window, thus avoiding the steep and narrow stairs in-side. As the chest was lifted up, Louise saw two sets of initials lovingly carved on the side of the box, just above this year's date, 1654. Newly-marrieds just moving in, surely. She shivered slightly. They waited until the chest was safely inside the window before walking on.

At the end of the street, the brick wall of the town defences rose in front of them. They found some steps that led to the ramparts above. The steps were steep, built for soldiers, and there was no balustrade, but Louise had a good head for heights, so she gathered her cloak and skirt in one hand, and climbed with the other touching the wall. Delicate tresses of what looked like ivy, but with pretty violet-shaped flowers, trailed from cracks in the wall. She picked a sprig and carried it with her.

She arrived at the top, leaned against the parapet and drew in great gulps of air, cleaning her lungs of the stench of the town and the stagnant odours of the canals. When Pieter arrived she asked him to pin the little sprig of flowers to her cloak and was surprised at how delicately he used his fingers. Immediately below the wall flowed the Schiekanaal, a slow river that embraced the town protectively on three sides. Beyond it the lowlands stretched as far as the eye could see. Above them towered great masses of cloud: white and silver and grey against the unbelievable blue of the sky. The dotted farms, windmills and distant spires seemed to be sailing along like ships in a smooth green ocean as the drifting cloud shadows passed. She looked over at Pieter, wanting to share her feeling of freedom. He was leaning forward against the wall, looking at the scene through tightly narrowed eyes. She imitated him, her lids drawing closer and closer together until the view became fuzzy and indistinct, reduced to essentials.

'It's like an oil painting,' she said, smiling at her

discovery. 'I'd have tried to paint every blade of grass, but you can't, can you?' She watched him while he opened his eyes and blinked.

'No, but there are some that try.'

'Wouldn't you like to be out there?'

'In the meadows,' he paused and then smiled. 'Chasing maidens?'

'No!' Louise protested, but she could feel a blush rising in her cheeks.

'Don't worry, that was his idea,' he laughed.

'He was just teasing you, wasn't he?' The boy smiled. She added wonderingly, 'He was teasing me too.'

A sailing barge, heading north for Leiden, passed by silently, its brown, tanned sail blocking out the view for a moment. The bargee's wife was cooking on a small charcoal stove. A delicious smell of frying onions wafted up to them. The bargee saw Louise looking down at him and waved. When his wife said something sharp to him he looked away with a grin. 'Is the Master always like that at the beginning of a picture?' Louise asked.

The Empty Glass

Chapter 5

Though Pieter had known the rich and famous from his work, he had never crossed the social divide that separated real wealth from humble employment. His father had been a valued painter in the DeVries Pottery, but there had been invisible barriers to his advancement on account of his religion. When it came to Pieter's apprenticeship, his father had joked that he would not apprentice him to the potteries, as he would break more pots than he could paint, but the real reason was his own frustration. When Master Haitink agreed to take on the boy as an apprentice, Pieter's father had urged him to strive towards becoming a member of the Guild of St Luke. 'Catholics are accepted there, Pieter,' he said. 'There is no barrier if you have the skills to prove yourself.'

But Pieter had no social ambitions. When his father died the following year, he willingly took on work in the Mistress's bar to help support his widowed mother. Life and ambition had not prepared him for finding himself on the walls of Delft with the town's richest heiress. He felt the presence of the girl beside him like a flame, as if she might burn, or blind, or – heaven forbid – blow out like a candle if he did the wrong thing. He found refuge in the view over the walls and squinted, watching the slow march of a cloud over the fields. The spring crops were above the ground now, oats, and wheat, and barley, each strip and chequer different. He watched the shade creeping forward, absorbing the delicate spring colours, creating a momentary gloom, and then releasing them in joy as it passed. Her voice broke his reverie.

'Master Haitink was leading me on, about the planets and Aristotle, wasn't he?' She paused. Pieter didn't know how to reply. 'But was it unseemly … my arguing with him … with your master? Father says that we must never undermine the beliefs of others, just say what we believe ourselves. But I ended up arguing with him.' She appeared to think for a moment. 'The trouble was, he was so like Annie, my old nurse, except that I whenever I try to discuss things with her she goes all prune with disapproval.' Pieter watched her undo her head-cloth and shake her hair free. The string of pearls that the Master had loosened slipped from the coils and trickled down her back like water. He stooped and picked them up; she didn't appear to notice. The tiny pearls slipped through his fingers while she gazed out over the meadows, lost in thought. Then, smiling to herself, she turned, eyes dancing.

'But he did go for me, didn't he?'

'He didn't stand a chance!' Pieter laughed. He wanted to tell her that the Master owned a modest spyglass and was, he was sure, as avid a follower of Galileo as she was herself, but he was afraid that she might not understand. The Master's deception had been in search of another truth, but how do you explain the work of angels? Now her face had clouded again, and he noticed how her eyes changed colour with her mood, blue-grey to green, like sunlight on a windy sea.

'Is he always like that,' she asked, 'clowning and arguing? It was almost … I don't know … as if he was frightened of me.'

Pieter, who had been thinking of sunlit seas, laughed and said, without thinking: 'Oh, he was, mistress, he was terrified.'

She opened her eyes wide. 'Me? How could he be terrified of me?'

'Because he was afraid that he could not paint you.'

'But that's ridiculous! He … he's *the Master*!'

'No, it's not ridiculous. People think that just because you're a painter, you will always be able to capture what you see on paper or canvas, but it's not like that at all. Often your eyes see things that don't seem possible to put on paper. When you take up your charcoal, or your brush, there seems to be no connection between your eyes and your hands. It was like that with the painting of the Beggar at the Begijnhof gate that you liked. We had to smuggle the old man up the stairs in case Kathenka saw him. At first it just wasn't working and the Master was like a bear. Then one day we got the beggar a little tipsy and he began to sing. Can you imagine that heap of rags pouring out love song after love song? He was like a canary in a cage. You wouldn't know from the portrait that he was singing, but it could not have been painted otherwise.

'But I didn't sing, all I did was argue,' Louise pointed out. She thought for a moment. 'Does this ever happen to you? That you can see but not get it down? I can't imagine you as a bear.'

'Yes ...' he said, surprising himself.

'Oh, do tell me.'

'But it's a silly example.'

'Go on, please,' she asked eagerly. Pieter paused to gather his thoughts.

'It was the first time that the Master had let me work on a live canvas. It was a routine portrait of a town councillor, and the Master had got bored with both the man and the painting. "I need some colour here, Pieter. Run down to Kathenka and get me a glass of red wine." I started down the stairs. "In one of the plain Venetian glasses," he called after me. I returned, carrying the wine carefully up the stairs. He placed it in the composition. "On second thoughts, Pieter," he said, "you will paint it." Now this was a real honour for me. He showed me where to place the glass in the canvas. "There, we will paint it just beyond the old scoundrel's reach." Then he chuckled and shuffled off, for the taproom, I suspect.'

'How did you get on?' Louise asked.

'Oh it was good! The glass appeared flat on the table, which is always a good start, but it was the wine that pleased me most. I had built it up in layers and had remembered from the beginning to leave one point uncovered so that when it took a final coat there was just a small ruby of red light glowing in its heart. When the Master came back I couldn't restrain myself. "Look, Master. Have you ever seen a finer glass? No need for you to go to the taproom; you could just reach out –" Thump!' Pieter laughed ruefully at the recollection. 'And I was lying on the floor looking up. It was the jibe about the taproom that did it. He is strong. He put a foot on my chest to keep me there. He took up the glass of wine, which had been my model, and drank it down in three gulps. Then he stood, polishing that glass with his cravat – his foot still on my chest – till the glass shone. When it was polished to his satisfaction he put it down on the table, tucked in his cravat, took his foot off my chest, and said, "Draw that!"'

'Were you hurt?' she asked.

'Mistress, I was not hurt, but I was hopping mad. Ten minutes before, you see, I had thought that I was a rival to the great Rubens himself, now I was being buffeted around like a first-year apprentice, and being asked to draw an empty glass … of all things! Well, I drew in the outline of the glass, checked that it was true – I didn't want another buffet – and called out, "Master, it's done." He waddled over. You should have heard what he said.' Pieter shook his head. 'Dear God, how I came to hate that glass, Louise. How he harassed me! I tried it again and again.

'"It's not one of your damned saints, you nincompoop!" he said at last. "Look … look … look … what's that?" He was jabbing at my page. "It looks like a bloody halo?"

'But master, that's the *rim!*' I said it through clenched teeth. 'See – it's there!

'"No, it is not there!' This time his thump set my ears

ringing. "Look with your *eyes*. How do you really see that rim?" I blinked and squinted because my eyes were watering from the blow; I was near to tears. And you know, Louise, at that instant I saw what he meant! The glass, the rim, it wasn't bound by lines at all, but by tiny unattached fragments and facets of light. The imagined glass that my mind had been trying to force on to the page had dissolved. Now I was seeing the glass with an artist's eye, albeit a watering one.' Pieter paused. He had been getting carried away, his hands, obeying him for once, were drawing the glass for her in the air between them. She urged him, with a gesture, to go on.

'It was as if I had made this great discovery all on my own. I said, "I see it, Master! Look, no rim … just two slender moons of light where the rim should be. You are right!"

'"Well, draw them!" he growled.

'For another hour I drew, while he lumbered up and down the studio like a bear shaking its chain. My sketchbook filled with these tiny meaningless fragments and shards of light. They floated over the page like forgotten dreams. Then, just as the light was going, the glass appeared. Oh, Louise, joy!

'"Master!" I shouted, and I looked down at my book in case it had flown away. But it was still there, a floating, translucent glass, captured on the page. I couldn't believe it! I sat back with a groan of sheer exhaustion. He stood over me, growling. I wanted to hug him then, but all he did was grunt: "Kathenka has opened a new cask, it has been calling to me this last hour. Come on, let's celebrate."'

Pieter stopped, dazed by his own eloquence. He was staring at the girl, seeing her with a painter's eye, much as he had looked at that glass. Not binding her with lines, but catching her essence as tiny unattached fragments and facets of colour and texture and light. He shrugged, and his hands flapped loosely.

Louise turned for a last look over the town walls. She must go home now. The rebelliousness that had brought her up here was being overtaken by a feeling of regret, she wasn't sure for what. She felt Pieter's eyes on her, but they weren't intrusive, they were soothing, like when the Master had patted and straightened her clothes ready for her sitting. The boy was an artist, and she was learning that artists looked at things differently to other people. She had watched him, seeing how he changed when he talked about his art, how his hands suddenly found co-ordination and became storytellers. For some reason she found his vision both disturbing and exciting; it was like being offered a forbidden fruit. Up till now she had believed passionately in science. Father described science as being like a new sun, burning away the mists of superstition and folly. Newer and more wonderful things were being discovered daily, not by mystics with woolly visions, but by mathematicians, and astronomers, and alchemists. If something could be measured, it could be believed. Now Pieter was offering her something different; it was new, and it was a little exciting, and a little shocking, but she wasn't sure what it was.

She was looking forward to Father coming back from Amsterdam tomorrow. Since she had been little, whenever Father returned from one of his trips – Amsterdam, The Hague, even abroad – he would come up to her room when she went to bed in the evening, and tell her of all the wonderful people he had met and the things he had seen. 'One day,' he would say, 'you will come with me.' Then they would plan exotic trips in which they met philosophers in gowns, and alchemists in pointed hats bent over bubbling retorts in search of gold and the philosopher's stone. She'd stay awake for hours after these sessions, her mind and pulse racing.

Then there was their telescope; the barrel was ready, beautifully crafted by the cooper from the pottery. All it needed were the lenses that Father had ordered from a lens grinder in Amsterdam. Then they would be able to see the moons on Jupiter … and perhaps even see the arms on Saturn. She wondered if Pieter would be excited by things like this. At one time she had thought that Reynier would be interested. He was, and she was delighted, but in the end she realised it was just so that he could create a new illusion: *Reynier, the man of science.*

And now there was this boy who spoke to her about art in a language she could understand, of 'fragments and facets of light'. Wouldn't it be nice if they could be friends? But she closed her mind; she was learning to shut some thoughts out. It looked as if her mind had been made up for her by society, and that she had somehow walked herself into her own destiny. She watched a heron flap heavily up the canal below them, its snake neck tucked tight between its shoulders. She watched its neck uncoil and its legs reach out, clawing at the water as it landed in the shallows. It was time to go. She turned to Pieter with a smile and held out her hand.

'Pieter, you have been very patient, but I would like a hand down the steps, I am trussed like one of those poor chickens in the Markt.'

He took her right hand in his and descended backwards, enabling her to hold up her cloak and skirt in the other. For someone so naturally awkward he managed well; she only had to stop him falling once. They paused to laugh. Suddenly the thought that had been teasing her swept through her mind like the flight of a swallow.

'Pieter,' she said, trying to keep hold of the thought.

'Yes?'

'When you drew your empty glass, you drew it as you knew it was, as your reason told you, and it looked all wrong?' Pieter nodded. 'So it was only when you forgot about reason and drew what your senses told you was there, that the glass appeared?'

'Yes, I hadn't been using my eyes.'

'But Pieter, that is not allowed. Our philosophers tell us that what we grasp with reason is more real than what we grasp with our senses.'

'Oh, dear. Does that mean that I got a clip over my ear for nothing?'

Louise laughed out loud, and the laugh echoed between the high wall and the gables of the town. She listened to the echo; it was an unexpectedly happy sound. 'No, the oppo-site, just wait till I tell Father. Pieter Kunst has just proved that our greatest philosopher is wrong.'

'Oops.' Pieter wobbled; she steadied him.

'It would be a terrible waste if you fell off, you know. You must be preserved; you are my forbidden fruit. Brace one hand on the wall as I did coming up.' They arrived, still laughing, at the bottom. Louise took Pieter's arm and they walked along in the shadow of the wall and she told him about her father and the telescope that they were building. Then she told him about the philosopher her father had met years ago.

'He lives ... no, lived ... in The Hague,' she said. 'Father was a bit in awe of him I think,' she smiled. 'He said just what I said to you there on the steps: what we grasp with reason is more real than what we grasp with our senses.' Louise looked up, a pale daytime moon was hurrying apologetically from cloud to cloud as if it had been caught out late. 'He said our senses pretend to us that there is a moon up there, and we believe that it is real, like the wall here, but we don't know. Perhaps it is really is a cheese, like we saw in the Markt, or perhaps we are seeing it in a dream and later we will wake up and it won't be there. The only way we can be certain that something is real is by reason.'

'Well, it didn't work for me. Reason told me that the glass I was trying to draw consisted of two ellipses, joined top to bottom by a number of curves, but when I drew it that way it looked like a tipsy saint with a halo.'

'But would it have worked if you were to measure everything? You see, Father says that that is how science works.'

'There is a method we have, using lenses and mirrors, that throws an image of what we want to paint on to the canvas. We use it, but not a lot. The Master says it is like the plan of a building before the house is built. It has no soul; that is something that has to be added.'

'Soul ...' Louise echoed. 'Perhaps that's the trouble with science, perhaps it has no soul.'

'But you love science, don't you? I can hear it in your voice when you talk about it.'

'Yes, oh yes, Pieter! To understand the universe as it really is. Maybe soon we will be able to discover the very keys of life, and we will be able to put right all the things that have been done in ignorance or in folly!' She paused. 'But I think there is something missing, Pieter. You called it soul. Somehow I'm not sure that there is room for "soul" in science.'

The Watch

Chapter 6

They walked side by side until they could see the Huijbrechtstoren, a rampart tower, standing over the wall to their right. Then they turned left towards the Doelen, the town shooting range, and passed the gunpowder store. It was a peaceful part of town, overhung by massive trees. Orchards and allotments stretched out to the curve of the town walls and the Schiekanaal. It was here that Louise's father had bought one of the new houses, attracted by the peace and quiet away from the busy town centre. There was grass beside the road so their approach to the gate of the powder magazine was quiet. A sudden movement caused Louise to grip Pieter's arm. It was Claes, watchman at the powder store, hastily putting something in his pocket. He smiled, but it was a shifty smile. Louise felt uneasy. She shivered and drew Pieter closer.

'That smelled like tobacco,' Pieter said, sniffing. 'I hope he doesn't smoke inside.'

'Oh, it would be forbidden. They even have to wear cloth shoes in case of sparks.' Louise reassured him. 'He'll be careful enough, he'd be the first to be blown up.' She looked ahead. 'Oh, look. They're coming out of the firing range now, let's walk quickly.'

A door had opened in the wall ahead of them and, in a clatter of armour and equipment, officers of the watch, who had been at practice, were spilling out on to the road. Louise held Pieter's arm firmly and lowered her head. She rather wished she had put on her head-cloth. There was a time, not long ago, when she would have joked and teased with the men. They were usually in good spirits, talking loudly from temporary deafness, faces scorched and black from having expended quantities of gunpowder on targets, or sweating from crossing swords in practice. One or two of them called greetings. She recognised Dirck van Vliet, the new captain of the watch.

'Miss Louise ...' the "Miss" was new; Louise did not reply, and then regretted it. She hadn't meant to be snooty. One of them called out to Pieter that he was parched, and was there anyone left at home who could give him a drink? Pieter made some reply that Louise didn't hear, because she was listening to another voice, unconsciously loud from the shooting range.

' ... DeVries, you know.' Reynier's surname fell on her ear like a ball of lead. Her face flushed; she had to force herself not to walk faster. So, she thought, it really is all around town. Even the town guard are linking our names. How, how, how had she let it happen? She was gripping Pieter's arm cruelly, but a gap seemed to be widening be-tween them already. Pieter – the humble apprentice – where did he stand in a community which seemed to be working itself up for the marriage of the decade. Her marriage! She couldn't believe it. She began to walk faster, but a group from the watch fell in with them. When she arrived at her house she almost grabbed her house shoes from Pieter. The jovial company stood in the road admiring the new house while Louise knocked on the door. She remembered Pieter and turned to thank him, but he had disappeared. The door opened behind her and the men in the road doffed their plumed hats. She turned and came face to face with Annie, who stood there, a look as black as a bible on her face. One glance was enough for Louise; she could not face Annie in a mood of righteous anger. She stepped quickly out of her clogs on to the cool of the marble floor. She had expected Annie to move to one side to close the door behind her, then she would make a dash for the stairs. But Annie knew her Louise. Instead of closing the door, she abandoned it and backed down the hall, blocking her way. Louise could still hear the loud voices of the watch outside. She turned, closed the door, and stood at bay.

'And who are those monkeys you have acquired? And where have you been? Flaunting yourself about the town?' Annie hissed.

'You know them as well as I do, Annie; they are the officers of the watch. Not monkeys, but gentlemen.'

'Shame on you, you hussy. Don't you realise that *gentlemen* are the last people you should be consorting with in your condition!'

'Annie! I'm not pregnant!' Louise exploded, half-laughing in frustration. 'And I'm not –' But Annie was not to be laughed at. She changed direction.

'How dare you sneak away without telling me!'

'I'm not in any special condition, Annie,' Louise persisted.

'Stop saying "I'm not". You are. What I want to know is how you sneaked out without my knowing.'

'You were talking to Mistress Kathenka,' Louise answered, dodging a lie like a skater skirting rough ice.

'Why didn't you call to me then?'

'There was no need; you were enjoying yourself.' At last Louise had got a shot home. For all Annie's puritanical zeal she did have one weakness, and that was a penchant for a 'little glass'. Some of her own carefully guarded cordials, though innocent to look at, were surprisingly potent. Louise had noticed a slender glass beside Annie's hand on Kathenka's table; Louise capitalised on this. 'Also Annie, I had an escort home: Mr Kunst.'

'Mr Kunst!' Annie snorted. 'An apprentice!'

'That's right Annie – at least he wasn't a *gentleman*.' It was time to go. You didn't score two shots against Annie and wait to see the effect. Louise slipped past her and ran lightly up the stairs. She felt a surge of relief, joy even. To-morrow Father would return from Amsterdam. Tomorrow she would tell him everything. Her mind was clear and her answers simple.

No, she did not want to be Reynier's wife. A business deal was a business deal and Father would never want her to marry someone she wasn't sure about. Everything had changed for her today. In the Master's studio she had found something new and exciting, something that Reynier could never begin to understand. She had thought of him as a protector, but now she could see his protection turning into bars for her prison cell. Perhaps she should feel guilty for having led him along, but how could she be involved with someone who would never understand people like the Master, Mistress Kathenka, the apprentice? People who stretched one's mind like India rubber. No, she would not marry Reynier DeVries.

She wasn't hungry. Annie would leave her alone. Mother was in bed, and Father was in Amsterdam. She climbed into her box bed, pulled the curtains that closed the little *bedstee*, and went to sleep curled up like a dormouse.

It was dark when Louise first woke. The house was quiet. Even the creaks and snaps made by the new wood as it adjusted to the changing temperature had ceased. She felt battered but refreshed, her mind floating clear. For a time she just lay there, looking up towards the ceiling of the box bed, and wondering if she would fall asleep again. Then she drew back the curtains, slipped out, draped a rug over her shoulders, and tiptoed to the window. The outside shutters were thrown back against the wall and the windows were folded in. She rested her elbows on the windowsill and breathed the night air. The dark hung in front of her, black as an unmarked slate. This is my slate, she thought, and I won't let anyone write on it: not Annie, not Reynier ... nobody.

Gradually she began to make out the outline of the trees

about the powder store. From far away she heard a song ...
a nightingale? No, a blackbird. Then the bird faltered,
considering perhaps whether it had woken too early. She
held her breath. There it was again! A little more confident
this time, a call that ran its course. She imagined the bird,
way out there to the east, cocking its head and wondering if
the sun had heard it, and if it should call again. It was in full
song now, and other bird voices were taking up its lead.
The sound swept closer and closer, until it poured like a
wave over the town walls. Only then did the wise old
thrush that lived in the trees about the powder store follow
the blackbird's lead and raise its head and sing its heart out.

Louise looked about in surprise; the tender green leaves
on the trees still hid their colour, but daylight had come. The
old thrush was beginning its song again; theme and varia-
tions. 'Yes, old bird, I heard you,' she said and stretched.
Then she clasped her hands and held the world in the circle
of her arms. She imagined the wave of birdsong sweeping
on around the globe; in a minute it would reach the sea.
Then what? It would leap the water to the islands beyond, to
England, and Ireland, and then on out over the silent seas.

I will be true. I will be true to myself, she promised. I will
tell Father that I do not love Reynier, that it is all a mistake.
He will understand. I don't want to marry anyone. We will
make our telescope together and explore the stars and he
will tell me about his philosophers. And Pieter will come
and he can tell Father about his empty glass. Then we will
take turns to look at the moons about Jupiter and see
Saturn's arms.

Goosebumps rose on her skin as the chill of the morning air seeped through her rug. She hurried back into bed and fell into a deep second sleep.

She was woken for the second time by the clatter of hooves on the newly paved road outside. To begin with, she listened with detached interest. There was often traffic to and from the allotments in the morning. Suddenly she was sitting straight up in bed. Those weren't cart-horses, they were riding horses. Father! She hopped over the board at the side of the bed, seized a light wrap from the back of the door, flew downstairs, and nearly collided with Annie on the landing below. Annie slept in what should have been Louise's bedroom, but Mother had felt that it was too much for the old nurse to climb the steep stairs, so Louise had happily taken the attic room for herself.

'Oh, Mistress Louise,' Annie called, 'you can't go down like that, Mr De –' but Louise was past her and away. She was already rehearsing what she would tell Father. The front door was still open as she came hurtling down the final flight of steps. Father stood in the doorway, outlined against the light. He was holding Mother, enveloping her inside his great travelling cloak. Too late, Louise noticed that there was someone else – a man – standing behind Father in the doorway. She faltered to a halt, her bare feet skipping on the cold marble.

'Louise,' Father laughed. 'You are like a bird looking for a place to land. Come … come to Father. I need a kiss from you, too.' He stretched out his arm like a heron's wing. Louise darted across the floor and felt it close about her protectively. She buried her face in his shoulder and breathed the smell of fine wool that has been wetted many times and as many times dried in sun and air. Father was home and everything was all right. Then she remembered the man at the door, and looked up, straight into the eyes of Reynier's father, Cornelis DeVries.

'I'll be off now, Andraes. We have a lot to think about and to plan. Till the great day, goodbye.'

The man turned and clattered down the steps. What? What had he said? What 'great day' was this? But Father was enclosing her again.

'Louise,' he said, 'I've got our lenses, and I have met a really *wonderful* man, I must tell you *all* about him.' Mother, nestling beside her, felt as light as a sparrow – two birds under the same wing. 'Oh, please God, spare her,' Louise prayed on impulse; they were all so happy together.

Back in her room, Louise dressed with care. Pieter had told her she would not be needed in the studio that morning, as they would be preparing it for her portrait. She had a dress from last summer, a bit faded, but it was yellow and spring-like. Father liked yellow. She added a blue over-skirt, which she then tucked up at her waist. This was for Annie, to show that she was also prepared for sober work. She hung her new green silk near the window where it could freshen up and the creases could shake out. Then she ran downstairs, hungry for news and for breakfast.

She heard his voice as she reached the door of the dining

room and hesitated, listening. Father was talking about his trip home from Amsterdam. 'I stayed with the barge as far as Leiden. The breeze had all the windmills spinning, they made the town look exactly like a centipede crawling along.' Her mother's rare laugh tinkled. He saw Louise hesitating in the door. 'Come on in Louise ... breakfast.'

From the array of food on the sideboard Louise helped herself to bread, some slices of meat, cheese and a mug of small-ale. Father was still detailing his travels, 'I had to over-night in The Hague on business and met Cornelis there.' He paused, was he looking at her? She didn't turn around, she wanted to hear more. 'So! Am I to expect a visit from young Reynier when he gets back, Louise?'

This was the moment to tell him, to get it over with. She turned; Annie was looking at her. No, not here ... this was private; it was between Father and her. She sat down, pretending not to have heard, but her face flared. She could feel their eyes on her: Annie's, Mother's. The moment was slipping away. Why was she so impotent? Then Father said, 'All in good time! All in good time,' and the opportunity had passed.

'Well, whatever,' Father went on, 'Cornelis is suggesting that we bring our two potteries together. It makes a lot of sense, you know. He will take over the tiles and tableware, while we in Eeden's will concentrate solely on the fine Chinese ware. Think of it,' he laughed. 'I'll never have to paint another blessed windmill!'

Louise stared at her plate, poking at the finely sliced ham. So, the plan really would be important to Father, not just a business deal. He had always wanted to be free to do this fine work. Father was the finest painter of Chinese designs in all Delft, but each pot took weeks to throw and paint. They commanded good prices, but it was the everyday Delftware that put the bread on the table. Louise's heart sank. Reynier had said this very thing, but she hadn't wanted to hear. And she could make Father's dream come true. All she had to do was say 'yes' to Reynier and she would be Father's fairy godmother.

There was a disturbance that Louise hardly noticed. The kitchen maid came in and whispered to Annie that Good-wife Drebbel was in the hall and wanted a word with her.

'Louise, did I ever show you the two pieces of original carrack porcelain that your grandfather bought fifty years ago, when the first boat came back from China? I have kept them hidden up till now, a little insurance policy to get me started if I ever had the chance to concentrate on the really fine ware.' The blood was pounding in Louise's ears. 'I will be able to copy these now. The designs alone are worth hundreds of guilders; I was afraid someone else might steal the designs if I produced them before.'

Why was he saying all this? Was he saying, 'thank you for giving me this opportunity'? For a moment the room dark-ened and she thought she might faint. How could he be so blind? He who had always seemed able to look into her mind and read her thoughts; surely he could see that he was breaking her heart? She'd let Reynier into her life in order to preserve space for *him*; she didn't want suitors, she didn't want Reynier, she wanted *him*. Now a new apprehension was growing; was this the norm, was this how all girls felt before marriage? Waves of panic, like the shivers that announce a fever, were chasing through her. She reached for a hard-boiled egg from the basket on the table. She raised her spoon and brought it down on the egg, only to gaze in disbelief at the mixture of crumbled yolk and splintered shell fragments in her palm. Father got up to assist Mother back to her room. Still Louise did not move; it was only when she heard his voice in the hall that rebellion boiled up inside her. It was *her* life, and nobody had the right to dictate it. She thrust back her chair.

'Father,' she shouted, blundering towards the hall. It was now or never. She pulled open the dining room door, but she was too late. She heard the street door slam. She wanted to run after him but Annie was blocking her way.

'You lied to me, you Jezebel!' Her old nurse was shaking with fury, like a peacock when displaying. 'Goodwife Drebbel has told me everything. It is one thing to sneak past me, but to parade yourself unchaperoned in the market place, to let young men kiss you like the whore of Babylon; it is a disgrace.' Louise felt her mouth opening and closing. At last she found her voice.

'But Annie, that was Rey –'

'No, it wasn't. Master Reynier left a week ago.' Louise shrugged; there was no arguing with Annie in this mood. 'And then who did you go off with?'

'I was accompanied by Mr Kunst; the Master charged

him with seeing me home.'

'And how long did it take him to do that?'

'I wanted to look over the walls, that's all. I've been cooped up all winter!'

Annie shifted her line of attack. 'How can you treat that poor boy like this?'

'Who, Annie?'

'Master Reynier, of course! It's bad enough being sent away just when your engagement should be announced.'

'There is *no* engagement, Annie!' Louise was almost shouting.

'You can't keep things secret from me; of course there is an engagement, he told me –'

'He didn't tell you. He told you that he was going away *because* of the rumours about us, you've got it all wrong.' But Annie knew better.

'Ever since you were children together he has looked after you.' She wagged her finger in Louise's face. 'And young *Miss* that you are, you accepted it!' That hurt Louise. 'Such a gentleman he's turned into, and such nice manners.'

'Annie, you've been trying to make us fall in love since we were in nappies!'

'Love!' The word almost exploded from Annie's mouth. 'What has love got to do with it? It is God that makes a marriage, not love.' Louise's heart sank, when Annie and God teamed up there was no stopping them. 'Do you think that God thinks only of Miss Louise Eeden? What about your father? His whole future is dependent on you. Everyone in Delft is on tenterhooks at the merger of the two great potteries.'

'But that is business, Annie!'

'Do you think then that God has no hand in business? Has he not guided the ships of our brave sea captains as they ploughed and sowed the oceans for the riches that make our nation great? Are God and business to be held at bay just because Louise Eeden refuses to bow to His will?'

Louise made one last bid for reason. 'But Annie, I'm not marrying a sea captain!' That was levity, and Annie's God was without humour. Her final blow struck home, low and hard.

'Think of your poor mother, Louise. Will she survive another winter like the last? Even now she coughs at night. I hear her, but you are too high and mighty in that attic of yours. Couldn't you let her see you married before she is gathered? Who knows what the Lord has prepared for her?'

Rage and tears rose like twin fountains inside Louise. Annie was right; Mother could not last. Louise had seen, but denied, those bright red spots of colour on Mother's cheeks that made her look so pretty; the terrible beauty of the consumption that was eating away at her from inside. But how dare Annie suggest that God would have anything but open arms and a loving embrace for Mother!

Annie stepped back from Louise and put her hand to her mouth, as if only now realising what she had said. She made an ineffectual gesture of appeasement as Louise thrust past her and thudded blindly up the stairs to her room. There Louise sat motionless, looking unseeing at the wooden panels on the wall and breathing through her mouth until it felt as dry as summer's dust.

The worst part was admitting to herself that Annie was right: right about Father, and right about poor Mother too. That comment of Annie's about Mother had been a slip of the tongue. Annie loved Mother – she loved them all – which was why she was so hard on them, and on herself too. Poor Mother, she had once been so strong, so gay, and so indestructible. When Louise was little, they would walk together out beyond the town walls, Mother laughing up into the wind, while her cloak billowed and her beautiful fair hair streamed behind her. Reynier would sometimes come too, but he seldom lasted more than the first broad field. Then they would be on their own, and while Louise picked wild flowers and jumped puddles, Mother would sing nursery rhymes and the folk songs of the Lowlands. They didn't talk much, but they shared the wonder of everything from the bright pink of the ragged robin, to the chestnut brown tufts on the lance-like rushes that grew beside it in those marshy places. They would wait patiently, hand in hand, for a butterfly to open its wings … peacock? … red admiral? Or they would spend long minutes following the rasping cry of a corncrake as it moved invisibly through the high meadow grass.

Then, one April, far from home, they both got soaked to the skin in an icy shower. Louise soon warmed up when they got back to the house, but Mother didn't. She went straight to bed and she stayed there; Louise was kept away. Eventually she evaded Annie's guard, crept into her mother's room, and slid into bed beside her. Resting her head on her mother's burning chest, she heard a crackle, like the rustle of dry tissue, accompanying every laboured breath. Spring passed; it shouted for Mother to get up and get better, but she remained in her room. Summer came and went. Gradually Louise came to realise that her mother was now an invalid and that their walks together in the countryside were a thing of the past. Louise was just ten.

She had to stop thinking for a while as she clenched her eyes against her rising tears. She took a deep breath and turned her mind deliberately to the subject of Reynier. As so often happened when she thought about him, her own inadequacies rose to the surface like bubbles from the canal. She was constantly at odds with Annie, while he always treated her with the most courtly respect. Annie pretended to disapprove, but in fact loved the attention. Thoughts of Pieter and what Reynier had said about him intruded – he really did look like a puppet, and he did get his strings crossed. She tried to remember how awkward he had been when they had climbed together on the walls, but all she saw were Pieter's hands drawing pictures for her in the air. A treacherous glow of happiness spread through her. *Verdorie nog aan toe* – don't be a fool, she told herself. This was ridiculous, comparing an acquaintance of a few hours to Reynier, whom she had known all her life. She closed her eyes and measured the words out in her mind. She *would* learn to love Reynier, for Father's sake, and to make Mother happy.

She opened her eyes. The wooden panels still stared blankly back at her, but inside she felt a brittle calm. She congratulated herself on the clarity of her thoughts. If Reynier repeated his proposal, as he surely would when he returned, she would accept him. Until then there was nothing she could do or say. She was certain now that the merger of the potteries depended on her, and she would do anything for Father's happiness. Mother's health would improve as the weather got warmer; she would tell her of her decision then. Louise considered the details of her plan; there was only one thing more that had to be done. She went over to her table. Her elegant little portable desk had become submerged under books, sketches for their telescope, and a homemade cardboard astrolabe that had collapsed. She pulled the desk forward. It opened down into a wedge-shape, sloped for writing. She unscrewed her inkpot, found a piece of crisp paper under the flap of her desk, inspected the nib of a rather chewed quill, and began to write.

I, Louise Maria Eeden ... She paused to think ... *do swear in the name of all truth, that, if asked, I will accept a proposal of marriage from Reynier Anthonie DeVries and will, until his return, hold myself as so engaged.*

She signed the letter, dated it: 21st April 1654, and stood up, wondering what to do with it. This was private to herself, but she wasn't equipped for keeping secrets. Her little desk certainly wasn't private. There was nowhere in her room ... then she had an idea. Inside the windows were shutters, folded back on themselves. She crossed the room and pulled at one of them. It stuck and then opened, releasing a smell of new wood and fresh paint. No one would have cause to open these until the bitter frosts of winter. Her note would have done its work by then. Resin was oozing from a knot in the timber. She pressed the note against it till it stuck, and then closed the shutter firmly. Even as she did so she heard a voice inside her head. *Six months of borrowed time, Louise,* it whispered, then added, *a lot can happen in six months.*

She had completed her pledge only just in time.

Lenses

Chapter 7

Louise got through the day, fortified by her new resolution and an unaccustomed feeling of virtue. Annie was a shadow of her usual self; her remark about Mother clearly weighed on her. For a while Louise rather enjoyed her discomfort and even tried a sniff or two, but scoring off Annie this way was no fun. Other people might apologise, but Annie could no more apologise than water could run uphill. In the end Louise had pity on her, waylaid her in the pantry, and gave her wrinkled cheek a quick kiss.

Evening came and virtue began to pall. She hadn't thought about Father, as that might mean thinking about that awful breakfast again. She was back in her attic and just beginning to feel that she should do something useful – like tidying her table – when the stairs creaked heavily. That was Father's step; there was a light tap on the door, and there he stood. He seemed hesitant, questioning almost, most unlike him. She was struck by how handsome he was. His beard was trimmed to a point, and his curving moustache swept up in a smile that asked to be reflected by a twinkle in his eyes. She tried to remember if Reynier's eyes twinkled, but his face had faded. All at once she knew why Father was uncertain; he was wondering if things had changed between them since the rumours over her engagement.

'Father,' she said, holding out her arms, and watched with pleasure as his face relaxed, the twinkle returned, and a mischievous look crossed his face. He stood there like a schoolboy with a stolen apple behind his back.

'Close your eyes and put out your hands,' he ordered. So she did. First a kiss – a brief brush on the cheek – then he placed a small but heavy cloth parcel in her hands. Her eyes shot open.

'Our lenses!' she exclaimed.

'Look at them, Louise. They're beautiful.' She unwound the cloth carefully. There were two packages inside, both wrapped in silk, one smaller than the other. She undid the bigger package. The silk slipped away and there it lay, in the lap of her dress, like a fish's eye, a beautiful glass lens.

'That's the objective – the big one,' Father said, as she held the glass up in wonder.

'But it's flawless, not one bubble. How do they make something so pure? It's like ice, there is not a speck in it.' She began to open the second package.

'Just be careful not to bang them together.'

'Will they fit our telescope?' she asked.

'The cooper has finished the barrel, and if my measurements are correct, yes. Baruch says that we should mount them in resin. If we have to adjust them then we can melt the resin and reset them.

'What's he like, this Baruch?' Louise asked. Father did not answer immediately, but looked out over the trees.

'Remember I said that I had met someone really amazing?'

'And it was he?'

'He's just a boy ... a Jew, but Louise, what a mind, what ideas! How I would like you to meet him.' Then he smacked a fist into his palm. 'I know, next time I go to Amsterdam, you will come too and you will meet him and ...' Here he stopped; Louise wondered why. He made a vague, dismissive gesture with his hands. 'Sorry Louise, I forgot. You will have your own plans, of course.' Louise seized him by his hand; it was rough from using clay. She wanted to bite it as a punishment. How dare he break their spell, but instead she kissed it.

'No, Father. Nothing will change. Whatever the future, we must go on doing things together. Of course I will come to Amsterdam and meet your little Jew.' Reynier had gone into solution in her mind; she couldn't even picture him. But she had made her decision and she would stick to it. Meanwhile she had her portrait to look forward to, the summer lay ahead, and the two lenses lay in her lap like crystal balls. She would introduce Father to Pieter and he would tell Father about drawing the empty glass, then she would travel to Amsterdam and meet Father's Jew. 'Now,' she said with determination, 'When will the telescope be ready? We will mount it here, in the window.'

'I'll bring these down to the pottery tomorrow.'

'Then you must tell me about our lens grinder, what was his name?'

'Baruch ... Baruch Spinoza, but later, Louise. I must go down to Mother now.' He kissed her and was gone.

Next morning, Louise stood at the studio door, amazed at the scene within. The curtains were drawn back and the whole place was flooded with light, but this was not the only change to the room. One whole corner of the studio had been transformed and she found herself looking into a room within the room. Even though it only had two real sides, it spoke to her. On the left was a table on which were books bound in leather; there was a globe and something that might even be a telescope, also some music manuscript. There was a bust, perhaps of Aristotle, and a stone urn with a panel awaiting an inscription. She got the impression of a tiled floor, but it was the rich Turkey carpet in deep blues and greens and reds that held her eye. On the carpet was a chair … her chair? It was turned from the table as if she had just got up from it.

She could hear Annie's laboured steps mounting the stairs behind her, but she could not take her eyes off the magical scene. To the right, defining the open side of the pretend room, was a little spinet, its painted lid lifted like a sparrow's wing. The back wall held a single picture, a sea-scape of barges with brown tanned sails all aslant on a choppy sea; a small guitar rested casually on the floor as if she had just put it down. She wanted to walk straight over and sit down, to take possession of the room and make its magic hers. Just then she felt a sharp jab in the small of her back.

'Don't stand in the doorway blocking the way for honest folk.' Louise stepped forward hastily as Annie, with solicitous support from Mistress Kathenka, arrived in the room. 'Oh for a chair! Why people don't bring their attics down to the ground floor like Christians, I just don't know,' said Annie, gasping. Then she saw the beautiful set-up in the corner of the studio, cried 'A chair!' and set off. Louise was rewarded with the strange sensation of seeing herself, aged seventy, plonking herself down in the middle of her own portrait. Since their altercation in the hall at home, and Louise's conciliatory kiss, Annie had changed. Louise wasn't sure why – perhaps she sensed that she had achieved her objective? Now seated, she glared around her. 'Mummery!' she said with acid disapproval.

Louise wondered what would happen next. Annie had insisted that she come to inspect the studio, and – though she did not say so – to inspect the Master as well. But where was he? Louise had been so taken up with the changes to the studio that she'd forgotten about him. On the way up the stairs she'd thought, with apprehension, that he might make some dramatic appearance: as the fencing master, a troubadour, or the hat-swinging clown. At that moment he did appear, moving from behind the open door of the massive paint cupboard. Louise saw Annie stiffen, her mouth pursing in anticipated disapproval.

The Master was dressed in sombre black. He had a simple linen cravat, such as pastors wear, around his neck, and he carried a small black book in his hand. He ignored both Louise and Kathenka and advanced on Annie to greet her with a short stiff bow. Annie was clearly taken aback. Louise guessed that she wasn't sure if she was being greeted by a suave devil or by a preacher. She stirred uncertainly, but the Master quickly signalled to her not to rise. Annie subsided, watching him warily.

'Welcome, sister,' he said. 'You must excuse this masquerade,' here he dismissed the transformation of the studio with a deprecatory flick of the wrist. 'It is just, shall we say ... what the occasion demands.'

Louise winced, then watched in fascination as Annie, her rock-hard, stone-cold Annie, begin to melt. The Master carefully placed a ribbon marker in his little black book and then turned to give her his full attention. 'Let me explain,' he began.

The thaw in Annie was not immediate; it commenced with defiant little movements of her hands and shoulders, but eventually Louise recognised Annie's complacent little smile. The Master must have spotted it too.

'Mistress Kathenka,' he said as if the idea had just struck him. 'I think we might bend the rule ... you know? A thimbleful of your special wine for our visitor, after the long climb?'

Kathenka curtsied and disappeared downstairs. She was back so quickly that Louise realised that she must have had the glass ready in the room below. She had to suppress a smile; all this was planned. The wine looked tempting, the colour of golden honey. 'So good for the heart,' assured the Master, in a voice worthy of a physician, and the last of Annie's inhibitions melted away.

During the course of the next half-hour the Master and Kathenka successfully negotiated for Louise to be available daily if needed, and to change, when necessary, in the privacy of the Mistress's room. In the event that Annie was unable to accompany her, the apprentice Pieter Kunst would ensure that she was escorted home in safety. Pieter was produced from the recesses of the studio. He was dressed in the garb of the humblest apprentice, and all but pulled his forelock for the old nurse. Annie appraised his status with care and clearly decided that he could be classed as a servant and therefore posed no threat to Louise's reputation. Louise also guessed that, as Annie assessed his looks, she decided that he would be no rival to the beautiful Reynier. When the wine was finished, with just a drop left for manners, Annie allowed herself to be guided out of the studio and down the many stairs, vowing – Louise hoped – never to have to climb these stairs again.

A silence fell in the studio. Louise suppressed a smile; she half expected the Master to ridicule poor Annie, who had so clearly fallen under his spell. But all he said was: 'A fine woman that,' and Louise was grateful. Only later, when he had shed his black coat and put on his smock did he allow himself a smile. 'Sometime, Mistress Louise,' he said, 'you should get Kathenka to give you a drop of that wine. It would melt the heart of Dr Calvin himself.'

Van Rijn

Chapter 8

The cooper had finished mounting the lenses and had departed, his face glowing from Father's praise for his work. The slender telescope rested on its tripod in the window of Louise's bedroom. She had insisted that this was the best vantage-point for viewing the stars. Evening light suffused the room. They turned the telescope onto the town walls, where a member of the guard was idly scratching his fleas. Then they looked at Louise's faithful old thrush, filling its throat for a song that seemed ridiculously faint and far away when it appeared that they could almost touch the bird itself. Then they probed out over the walls to the spires and the flickering windmills of the villages to the east.

'I wish it were dark, I can't wait to look at my first star,' Louise said. She patted the window-seat beside her, anything to prolong her father's visit. 'You promised to tell me about your visit to Amsterdam and the Jew who made our lenses. *Take me there.*'

Father laughed. 'You're too old for that now.' When Louise was little they had played a game where Father would recount his travels as if she was with him.

'No, seriously, tell it to me like you used to, as if we were off on an adventure together. I'm tired of being cooped up here in the town and … ' her voice trailed off into danger-ous territory. So she took his hand in hers and pulled him down. 'Remember, you used to say that I could almost read your mind. But perhaps there are dark secrets you don't want me to know about?'

'Secrets, perhaps, but not dark ones. It would have been better if you had been with me, but I'll try. Ready? Then take my arm, it's muddy along here.'

Louise closed her eyes and in a minute was imagining herself walking beside him. 'Where are we?' she asked.

'Amsterdam,' he said. 'When we cross this little bridge here we will be in the Jodenbreestraat. We are going to see a man called Rembrandt; he's a famous painter.'

'Is that the man Master Haitink calls van Rijn?'

'Yes, he prefers to use his Christian name; there are a lot of van Rijns, but only one Rembrandt. I wish I could have got him to paint you.'

'No, I like Master Haitink. He talks about van Rijn though; they were students together. Why are we going there?'

'We are going to see his collection of curiosities; you will enjoy these. His house is just at the edge of the Jewish quar-ter, so we can go there later to pick up our lenses.'

'Curiosities? You mean things like shells, and stuffed otters, and suits of armour?'

'Why yes, how did you know?' Father sounded surprised.

'Master Haitink has all of these things, and lots more, at the back of his studio, all higgledy-piggledy.'

'We will see birds of paradise with flowing tails in colours you can't imagine, Japanese armour made out of bamboo, and a Roman emperor or two.'

'Stuffed?'

'No,' he laughed, 'marble busts.' Louise smiled and wriggled close to him. The old magic was working; soon she would be free, living one of Father's adventures with him, away from the terrible claustrophobia of a winter behind town walls, and away from her own dark thoughts. She could picture herself now, a hand over his arm, walking beside him as he told her about the great painter's collection.

'There were samples of minerals, and a unicorn's horn, Venetian glass, and a wretched Chinese porcelain vase that he kept trying to sell me. People say he is in financial difficulties, but that vase was from a very poor pottery. I suppose he uses these objects for ideas, inspiration, as models to put in his paintings, but I missed ...'

'Missed?' Louise queried.

'I missed any real spirit of enquiry. All these wonderful things – a unicorn's horn, for that surely is wonderful! But to him they seem to be just things to have and to collect. I suggested that the horn was a whale's tooth, but he said that he had it from a man who had actually seen the fabulous beast. Then he began urging me to buy this "priceless vase" again, so I made my escape.'

'Into the Jewish quarter? What's it like?'

'It is just like the rest of Amsterdam – a mixture. But, oh Louise, the smell of baking! There was a bakery up near Rembrandt's house and I kept getting these delicious wafts of fresh bread. Our Amsterdam Jews,' Father went on, 'come from Portugal, so they have all their Portuguese trading contacts. They get sugar from the Americas; nuts and spices, dates and raisins from Africa and the Mediterranean. They speak Portuguese too, a soft lilting tongue, not hard and glittery like Spanish. But the smell of their cooking: cinnamon, cloves, spices, it nearly killed me. I found the bakery and bought us a big bag of biscuits.'

Louise felt her mouth water. 'Can I have one?'

'No, not now.' He chuckled. 'They are about to be eaten by Baruch, our lens grinder. He lives down near the old shipyards.'

'Alleyways?'

'Yes, but it has a different feel to the Dutch part of town where you think of people just ... well ... living, behind their doors. In the Jewish quarter you feel that behind every door there is business going on: transactions are being made, trade, workshops. Tailors sit in windows to get the light. Doors open and close, people come and go, and you get the impression that there is a different heart thumping away in there; it looks Dutch, but it's not Dutch.'

'And Baruch?'

'I found his door and knocked. I expected a bearded old man, but a lad who looked like an apprentice came to the door. I asked to speak with his master. He laughed then, and said he *was* the Master. He took me through to his workshop, to where he grinds his lenses. How anything so perfect as our lenses came out of that workshop I don't know. Dust from the grinding lies everywhere. I wanted to know –'

'…everything?' Louise interjected, adding, 'Poor Baruch.'

Father smiled sheepishly. 'Well, why not. He showed me the whole process: how he calculates the curvature of the lens and how he grinds and polishes the rough-chipped glass, wearing it away with finer and finer powders of emery.'

'Emery?'

'He says it is a mineral that is harder even than glass.'

'What does he look like? And how did he like being quizzed of his secrets by you, a mere Gentile, albeit a handsome one?'

'Jew, Gentile, what's the difference? He's twenty-one or two, dark, long hair – his own – no beard, straight nose, slight cleft in his chin, and very hungry.'

'For knowledge?'

'Yes, but chiefly for our biscuits.'

'I was afraid so,' said Louise wistfully. 'What did you talk about?'

'The lenses, astronomy, stars. We sat outside in his little courtyard, eating biscuits and sipping a heavy wine that he says comes from the island of Madeira.'

'May I have some?'

'I'm sure he would be delighted. Then we talked telescopes …' Father's voice trailed off.

'Yes?' Louise imagined herself in the sheltered courtyard, sipping a sweet, exotic wine. Eventually Father came back from some private journey of the mind.

'You remember, Louise, that time when you were small and we floated little reed boats in the rain barrel, and you noticed that if the water was really still, the little boats seemed to be pulled towards each other? It was like that between Baruch and me. It was as if our minds were speaking to each other but we had not yet found a common language. It got darker and darker in the little courtyard; a first star appeared in the wedge of sky above. Then he said: "Let's go up on the roof and I'll show you my newest telescope."'

'On the roof … like storks?' Louise laughed at the notion of the two of them balanced on one of the platforms that people built to encourage storks to nest on their roofs and so bring luck to the house. Father smiled.

'No, his house has two ridges with a valley in between. He has built a platform up there in the valley so that, apart from a chimney or two, he can see the whole of the night sky. Oh Louise, wait until you see. It was my first time using a real telescope, not a mere mariner's glass. How can I explain it?'

'Go on.'

'It is … it's like leaping upwards into clear water, rising through shoals of stars. I had always thought of the Milky Way as like a stroke of paint on the surface of the sky, but it's not, it is deep, it is made of myriad upon myriad of stars, all winking like phosphorescence disturbed in the wake of some celestial oar. I was almost speechless. "One more lens, Baruch," I gasped, "and I will be gazing on the face of the Creator himself!" He has a soft voice, Louise, like his Portuguese tongue, but it was what he said that shook me to the core.'

'Yes?'

'"Sir," he said, "There is no creator, that *is* the face of God that you are looking at."'

This time Father really had carried Louise with him. She felt as if she were on the roof beside them, listening to their conversation as they crouched at the telescope. Dare she interrupt?

'But Father, there *must* be a creator, we have a creation, therefore there has to be a creator.'

'No, my love, remember your logic, remember your Aristotle? That is a circular argument. It is only because we use the word "creation" that we say there must be a creator. Think, if we use a different word, Nature, say, to describe the universe, then it no longer demands a creator; we would just say that it was natural.'

'Well, someone made it!'

'No, you have watched frost growing on a window, you have seen the trees break into leaf; they have their inner purpose, but no one comands: "Leaf, grow here."'

'But if there is no creator, where is God? Have we lost Him?'

'No, my love, it is just that we have been looking for Him in the wrong place.'

'Explain.'

'Like this.' Father got up and tipped the telescope down; she thought he was going to train it on the road below, but instead he turned the tube around. 'Here, Louise, come and look at this.' She got up, 'Stand back a bit, don't put your eye too close.'

'I can't see anything. It's the wrong way round,' she murmured.

'Look in the middle. See, a small disc of light?' Then she saw it. There, miles down the tube, was a miniature picture. Something the size of an ant was moving in it. She looked up past the tube to identify what it was, and saw old Claes, from the powder store, searching back and forth for something on the road. She looked back down the tube. There were two things that looked like cabbages above the tiny figure. To her amazement she realised that these were the huge trees that overshadowed the Doelen.

'But Father, I don't understand! I can see what the telescope is doing, but who would ever use it this way?'

'Exactly. But I think that this is what Baruch says we have done with God. God gave us a telescope – our brain – to see him with, but we did not like what we saw: nature, human love, human frailty, freedom to think. This wasn't comfortable for us. We didn't want to get close to life; we wanted to get away from it. So we turned the telescope around and pushed God out to the safety of heaven, where we don't have to bother about Him.'

'So that means that God is really just out there, in the town of Delft.' Louise paused, tasting the new idea. 'He is everywhere!' An unexpected feeling of warmth spread through her. She smiled to herself. 'I like that,' she said, 'it seems right, doesn't it?' No wonder Father had been drawn to that strange young man. She was drawn to him herself. She reached out and gently pulled Father's beard. 'I had to do that,' she explained.

'Why?' Father asked.

'Just so I could say that I had tweaked the beard of God.'

Then with a laugh, she twirled away, avoiding his smacking hand, and spun around till her skirts flew out.

'You really liked him, didn't you. Your Baruch?' She said, as she spun back. Father took his time to answer.

'I don't know how long we spent, looking at the stars. Then we both just lay back against the warm tiles in the trough between the roofs and stared at the Milky Way turning silently overhead. It seemed to me as if he was working out his ideas even as we lay there. "I can *see* the answers," he said once, "I can *feel* them, but they are useless unless I can prove them." He has some crazy notion that he can prove his ideas, as if they were theorems in geometry.'

'And write QED at the end?' Louise suggested.

Father chuckled. 'I must suggest that to him, *as we set out to prove.* You see, Louise, you and I may seek the face of God, but Baruch Spinoza wants to cut steps in rock for us to follow.'

Cupid

Chapter 9

On her next visit to the studio, Louise did not put on her green dress. Kathenka took it away carefully in its linen bag, to hang in her room ready for later sittings. At last Louise was able to sit in the chair that had been set so invitingly for her and to look around. When she sat down she realised, almost with disappointment, that the 'room' was not as real as it had appeared at first sight. What she had thought were tiles in the floor were just strings criss-crossing under the Turkey carpet. She asked Pieter about them and he laughed.

'We will paint these in as tiles; attic boards would not be appropriate in the room of a "lady of science."' He was teasing her, but it was nice teasing. It didn't make her feel inadequate as Reynier's teasing so often did. 'We will have to make the windows grander too,' he said. 'Stained glass, probably; they must balance the spinet on the other side. You must choose what sort of tiles you would like on the floor.'

'Oh, black and white marble, please,' she said, thinking of the hall in their new house. 'But it is all so much work ... so much preparation, just for me.'

'Oh no, it really is important; the room, the furnishings, all must help to make the portrait. These things give messages about the subject of the portrait, symbols if you like, that hint at the subject's interests and even desires.'

'Desires?' Louise asked, suddenly on the defensive; then instantly regretted it. He looked so stricken, as if he were about to come apart at the joints.

'Well, sometimes we use what we know,' he was flushing deeply. 'The picture on the wall, for example – we tried a map, but it looked too gloomy, what with the globe and the books. Then Master suggested that,' and he pointed uncertainly to a picture of a cupid, complete with bow and arrow, that was leaning against the wall. 'But Kathenka said not. Then I thought of how the clouds had moved over the fields when we were up on the walls and I thought of the sea, so we borrowed that seascape from the Master's room. It's by Van Goyen.' He smiled at her uncertainly, his hands turned out.

She looked at him, remembering their time on the walls. She felt her colour rising and looked away. What was so attractive about this shambling youth, she wondered. She looked at the picture again. It was a seascape of greys and greens, broken only by the angular geometry of brown sails.

'I like it,' she said, but hoped that they would move Cupid to somewhere else.

Father had left for the pottery, and the house seemed quiet and empty after his departure. Louise had done the chores that Annie insisted on her doing so that she would not become 'spoiled'. Then she went, as she usually did, and sat with Mother for a while. It was Reynier who had sown in Louise the notion that she might have been responsible for her mother's ill health.

'You really mustn't blame yourself,' he had comforted her. 'Your poor mother could have been caught in a shower at any time.' It hadn't in fact occurred to Louise that she might be to blame, but her ten-year-old mind was fertile ground for such suggestions, and she *had* delayed, looking for frogspawn. Even after all these years a feeling of guilt welled up in her as she held the translucent hand that rested on the covers. She longed for someone in whom she could confide; it had been such a relief unburdening herself to Kathenka. The trouble was, that after her discussions and arguments with Father, the girlish chatter of her friends about clothes, and hats, and ribbons seemed vacuous and boring. When they wanted to talk about boys they didn't include her, as they automatically paired her off with Reynier.

As Mother declined, Annie had assumed responsibility for Louise's day to day life. It was a curiously lopsided upbringing. Once Louise had completed her tasks about the house, Annie would feel that her duty was done. From then on, Louise was largely left to her own devices, and would wander the town, making friends with anyone who would talk to her, pestering them with questions about anything from windmills to brewing ale. In only one other area did Annie try to exert her influence, and that was in religion.

She was a strict Calvinist for whom God was a grim reality. Father, on the other hand, would insist that Louise make up her own mind: 'You can only believe the believable, my love,' he would say, and in doing so he would quietly undo most of Annie's efforts. However, there was one faith which Annie abhorred above all others: Catholicism. Here she gave no quarter, would listen to no argument, and was not above subterfuge. And she fought her case with facts. Many a night Louise's bedtime story would be some gruesome detail of the Spanish Inquisition. If Louise had been naughty, she would be stood up in her window, which looked south, and be reminded that the Spaniards were only a few miles away, in the Spanish Netherlands: "... and we all know what *they* do!" Louise was genuinely scared and told Father nothing about Annie's dire warnings.

Mother's cheeks seemed slightly less flushed today, Louise thought to herself, and her breathing was a little easier. But she tired very quickly, so, after settling her more comfortably on her pillows, she left her mother to her rest and went downstairs.

Louise was restless and bored. She tried her lute, but it was out of tune – again – and when she carried it to the spinet in the parlour she found that that too was out of tune. Perhaps it was the lingering damp from the new plaster in the house. Her mind kept turning to the studio. Would it be very forward to go there without being asked? Eventually, her mind made up, she told her mother that she was going to the studio and was soon hastening through the sunlit streets to the Markt. Here she paused to get her breath back.

She looked in on Kathenka, with the intention of asking her if it would be all right to go up, and then stood shifting from one foot to the other, offering to help her clean the bar, but hoping not to be taken up on the offer. Kathenka sent her off upstairs with a knowing smile. At the top of the stairs Louise tapped at the board door and listened for an answer. She inhaled the studio smells as they filtered through the door. She recognised linseed oil; that was used for mixing the paint, and then there was the sharp clean smell of the turpentine they used for thinning paints and cleaning brushes. Someone was hammering inside. The noise stopped, and she knocked quickly before it could start up again. This time the Master's voice called out.

'Come in!'

She opened the door. Pieter was balanced on the top of a ladder, hammering a nail into the wall. She remembered their unsteady progress down the steps from the town wall and hoped he would be all right. 'Ah, it is Mistress Louise.' Pieter swayed on his perch.

'Her room,' as she thought of it, now looked more like a spider's web. The Master, short and squat as a spider, was looking out at her from within a web of strings, while poor Pieter looked about as much at ease as a daddy-long-legs caught in the mesh. He emerged unscathed, however, and backed past her with a grin, paying out one of the pieces of string. He attached this to a pole, which, Louise guessed, represented the missing corner of the room.

'Come, my dear, come. Ignore Pieter; he was going to play your part and sit for me, but he is no jewel. Today we set the jewel in the crown. Come and sit down. We must make magic, and later I will explain to you the wonders of perspective.'

Louise adopted an approximation of her pose while the Master busied himself behind his canvas. She longed to see what he was doing. Sometimes he held up his paintbrush as if to preserve the angles of what he saw, sometimes he used a thread stretched between his hands. Twice he moved the easel. Then, when he was satisfied with that, he got her to move her chair to the right. 'No, no, too far.' Pieter came and knelt behind him. They conferred in whispers. At last he was satisfied.

'Now, my dear, you may come and look. Careful of the easel!' he warned, as Louise tipped one of its legs. 'From now on, even if the canvas is moved, your chair and the easel must stay exactly where they are. I will show you why.' The Master took her arm and guided her to where he had been kneeling.

'Here,' he said. She knelt down and stared at the canvas and tried to decipher what she was seeing. The Master's crude sketch of her head and body throbbed from the canvas but now it seemed to be encased in a criss-cross of straight lines. She could recognise the network of Pieter's tiles on the floor, but what were all these lines that appeared to converge on just one point, her right eye?

'Ouch!' she said. 'You've stuck a pin in my eye. Why have you done that?'

'Ah, so you've seen it. I hope it doesn't hurt.' The Master chuckled. 'Ja, my child, that is where you will be, there where all those lines meet. The pin is where your eye will be, and where all eyes will go.' He pretended to drop his voice. 'Pieter is too dumb to understand, of course, you realise.' Louise looked up. The boy was grinning. The Master went on. 'Pieter now, he would paint you here, in the middle ... but that is not Master Haitink's way. No, that is too obvious, too like a portrait. I want people's eyes to be *drawn* to you, but they must not know why. So I do with you what I did for the beggar at the Begijnhof gate. I put you in my secret place. Let me see if you can guess,' he chuckled. 'It is a place that is hidden to the casual eye, a place where all lines go but none are seen.' He stopped, one eyebrow raised, delighted with himself.

'It's a riddle,' Louise laughed. She could guess, but she wanted him to explain. 'Tell me.'

'Look,' he said, kneeling at the canvas with his back to her, 'look over my shoulder as I do this. I take my little thread and I stretch it from the pin. See, now it is parallel with Pieter's tiles – here, and here, and here; now it is following the skirting board, now the windows. These are all lines that appear to stretch away from us; they are the ones that deceive our eyes so that the room appears to exist inside the canvas. When these lines have done their work – as tiles, as skirting boards, or as windows – they stop. But what if we draw them on, where do they go? The answer is here, to our pin.' He swung the thread from line to line around the pin as he talked. 'This point is called the vanishing point. The point where all lines go but none are ever seen. That, my dear, is where you will be. Because it is to here that the eye is drawn, as surely as a dog is to a bone.'

'Now, my dear, your hand please, you must help me to get up.' Louise helped him to his feet. She noticed Pieter's amused expression as the old man dusted his knees. The Master glanced up: 'Look at him, idling as usual. Come, children, I have work to do.'

Toy Boats

Chapter 10

Weeks passed and Louise was happy. The Master seemed reluctant to start on her part of the portrait. He was, as he called it, 'blocking in' the base colours for the background, edging towards the charcoal lines he had drawn on that first day when she had frozen for him. Strictly speaking, she wasn't required, but, having done her chores, she usually contrived to call in at the studio. Sometimes the Master would get her to sit while he made sketches of her in his notebook, but she felt that he was doing this more out of politeness than anything. When she got up to go, he would growl at Pieter: 'Conduct Miss Eeden home, Pieter, and no dallying on the way back!' If Pieter wasn't ready, Louise would go down to help Mistress Kathenka in the bar or kitchen, or wherever she was needed. In that way it would happen that she was often still there when Pieter came down. Kathenka would then say that she would be happier if Louise had a proper escort for the short walk home. But the walks weren't always short. They would start out and, by tacit agreement, Louise would allow Pieter to walk behind her, in the role of disinterested escort, while in the public Markt. But once they were away from the crowds,

Louise contrived reasons for visits to the town walls, or walks down to the Oosterport, where they could stand on the bridge under the wide sky, breathing the air and escaping the feeling of being perpetually trapped behind high walls. As soon as they were alone she would take his arm and she would think again of her tiny reed boats and how they pulled each other together in the rain barrel; of Father and his Jewish friend, of herself and Pieter. The fact that she was drawn to Pieter was a scientific phenomenon, the fulfilment of a natural law. When she imagined lying back on sun-warmed tiles watching the heavens roll, it was Pieter, not Father or Baruch, and certainly not Reynier, who was the unseen presence at her side.

Leaning over the bridge at the Oosterport, she told Pieter about their new telescope. She found that he knew quite a lot about astronomy.

One day he said: 'It was when we were looking at the mountains on the moon through the Master's telescope that he told me how Galileo had destroyed Aristotle's theory of the heavenly bodies being perfect spheres.' Silence. Pieter turned. Louise was looking at him. Something about it made him uneasy. He blundered on: 'He n-n-noticed their shadows on the lunar surface ...' Louise put her hands on her hips and cocked her head to one side.

'Pieter Kunst!' she demanded. 'Do you mean to say that all the time the Master was arguing with me for the *divine truth* of Aristotle's outdated arguments, he was just pretending? Do you mean to tell me that you knew this, and that *you* looked on without saying a word while I, poor innocent that I was, was being so grossly deceived?'

Now Pieter really did look as if his strings had been cut. She half expected him to collapse into a heap of arms and legs. It was too much for Louise; she threw back her head and sent a peal of laughter speeding down the Schiekanaal that startled jackdaws into flight from the gatehouse roofs. A surprised member of the watch emerged from the gatehouse, saw her, and scratched his head. 'Oh Pieter!' she said, as a relieved Pieter re-assembled himself.

They talked about everything then: about astronomy, and painting, even about Spinoza and his strange ideas. Louise was never certain what Pieter really thought of these theories about God. He would ask her questions and even put her right when her arguments got lost in the sand. But when it came to his beliefs, his eyes would part-close, as they did when he was seeing pictures in his mind, and she would realise that he was thinking, as it were, with his artist's eye, and she didn't know how to follow him.

On one of their walks, they found themselves near the Begijnhof gate. Here they found the old beggar; he still remembered Pieter – and Kathenka's special brew – and greeted them like a king and queen. The streets were deserted as they made their way home. Louise slowed to let Pieter catch up. Then they both looked up at the leaning tower of the Oude Kerk. Puffy white clouds scudded across the sky and Louise gazed until it seemed that the clouds stood still, and the spire appeared to be tipping over on top of them. She fell back against Pieter, laughing, and let him hold her lightly while she blinked the illusion away. She glanced up at him and noticed that his eyes were far away, perhaps capturing the scene for some future occasion.

Thinking of the little boats jostling in the rain barrel, she asked, 'Pieter, do you like me?' It seemed such a simple question; she just wanted to know – part of her research into small boats. She was dismayed when a stab of pain crossed Pieter's face. The arm that was holding her stiffened until it felt like a piece of wood, and he politely returned her to her feet. When he spoke, his voice had a harshness and a tightness that she could not understand.

'Yes, Miss Louise. I like you very much, but you forget your situation; it is time that you were home.'

That night, Louise went over the incident again in her mind. What was it about her question that had affected Pieter so deeply, and what had he meant by 'her situation'? Could he mean Reynier? She fell asleep while pondering the answer.

~⚹~

Annie brought the letter in to her, and hovered while Louise opened it. 'It's from Master Reynier,' she said approvingly.

The letter ran to several pages.

My dear Louise, it began. *It grieves me most terribly that I was such a boor as to expect a kiss from you when we met in the Markt on the day I left. It was shameful of me to have presumed on our friendship like that in public, and in front of Pieter Kunst – a simple soul, I think you'll agree – but not really one of us. Forgive me please, I'm sure you understand.*

Louise felt her anger rising.

I felt I had been pressing you too hard, and then, from God knows where, came these uncalled-for rumours about our engagement. Whatever my desires, I have my duty. These rumours have put you in an intolerable position. I cannot return to Delft without declaring my passion, therefore I must absent myself completely. I was lucky enough to pick up a ship that was sailing for Italy, although I didn't really care where it was going. We arrived in Le Havre today, which is in France. In this way I take myself away from you and from temptation. Perhaps I will find distraction in the mighty Parthenon in Rome …

Louise blinked. This was a new height of eloquence for Reynier, but she had to smile. When, she wondered, would Reynier discover that the Parthenon was in Athens, and not in Rome? She was still smiling at the thought, when she looked up and caught the very satisfied expression on Annie's face. She sighed and finished the letter; it had taken some weeks to find its way from France. So, Reynier really wouldn't be returning until the autumn. She sat back with her eyes closed for a moment, a sensation of reprieve flowing through her. Italy seemed wonderfully far away. She could feel herself relaxing; a wicked little thought crossed her mind. She looked up at Annie, who was watching her complacently, hands clasped in front of her. Louise tucked the letter into her bodice.

'Annie,' she said, innocently. 'Reynier is off to the Mediterranean. It's stiff with pirates, you know. Can you imagine Reynier as a galley slave?'

'Oh! Mistress Louise!' The little nurse's face trembled. 'We must trust in God for his safe return. At least he'll be among Christians in Italy, even if they are Catholics.' Louise felt no remorse at teasing Annie; she had no right to stay watching her while she read Reynier's letter.

Since their altercation in the hall, they had reached a state of armed neutrality. Annie approved of the studio and the Master: 'such a courteous gentleman'. Pieter was conveniently dismissed as a mere servant, and Louise did her chores and divided her time between her mother's bedside and the studio. It was time for her to go there now. She bent to put her sewing things into her basket and then paused halfway as a thought struck her. How had Annie known that Reynier was going to Italy? She had mentioned the Mediterranean, but not Italy. Louise looked across at Annie, busily hemming a linen skirt, and wondered.

There was no answer to her knock. Louise eased the studio door open quietly and tiptoed in. They were both there, crouched in silent concentration over the canvas. It had been taken down from the easel and was propped on a sloping stand set on a bench where it got good light from the north windows. Louise could feel their intensity. She stepped across silently, and stood, enthralled, watching the

Master at work. Now everything he did seemed controlled and compact. She thought back to the sometimes hectic sketching that he had done on her first day. In his left hand he held, not just his palette, but a long polished stick with a pad on the end. Pieter had called it a maulstick, but she hadn't understood how it was used. Now she saw it as part of the slow rhythm of his work. First came the careful charging of the brush, hardly more than a whisker on a slender handle. Then, in a single, slow, precise movement, the Master would lean forward, and the padded stick would come to rest on the edge of the canvas. Using the stick to support his wrist, he would carefully feather in a tiny dab of paint and then rock back. She watched this metronome movement without stirring, until eventually the Master straightened himself.

'Ja! Pieter,' he announced triumphantly, 'we have the colour right this time. If Miss Louise were here would she not kiss the old man on the cheek in appreciation?' He cocked his head to one side expectantly. Louise didn't accept his invitation but clapped lightly. The Master sighed, 'Too old, too old. You try, Pieter.'

The work went on. Neither of them paid her the slightest attention after that. Only the occasional low-voiced consultation broke the silence; the quiet activity closed around her like a cocoon. She began to think of all her privileges: her new house, her wealth, the green silk dress that she had hardly worn, and she asked herself what she was doing to deserve all this? She thought with irony of her demand to be painted like the beggar at the Begijnhof gate when a tenth of what she would inherit could house and feed all the beggars of Delft for life. And also there was Father, who could be free to do his own fine work, like these two craftsmen, if the potteries merged. So that too was in her gift. She remembered also – a little guiltily – how Reynier was sailing on dangerous seas just to give her a chance to make up her mind about marriage to him. How could she atone for all this? If only she were Annie … Annie always knew what was right and what was wrong; God told her. The words of a recent sermon came to mind, 'Brethren, there comes a time when we all must make that leap of faith. Leap brothers, leap sisters, leap into the arms of God!' She *would* marry Reynier when he came back in the autumn. The time was shrinking, but autumn was still a long way away.

Day by day, Louise watched her face emerge from the canvas. It was as if she were inside the canvas, wiping an ever-widening spy hole in a frosted window and peeping out. She wanted to wink at herself. Her right eye appeared first, bright and curious. Gradually the spy hole in the frosted glass widened; another eye appeared, then an eyebrow. Things went well for a while. The Master would hum while he worked, and Pieter would be in attendance. If she wasn't sitting for him, the Master was happy to let her watch. But gradually the summer heat became oppressive. It bore down on them, and the atmosphere in the studio became uncertain. The Master would get her to sit long hours for him, but she noticed that even though he changed position, picking up brushes and putting them down, he often did nothing. Then, in a flurry of determination, he would charge his brush, lean forward, the brush would hover above the canvas, then his hand would fall to his side and he would sit back with a groan. The portrait was not going well. Her whole face had emerged now. There was no question about a likeness; it was the face that looked out at her each day from Mother's mirror in the hall. But it was lifeless; even she could see that – so like – but so lifeless.

The atmosphere in the studio was sometimes actually hostile. Her tap at the door would be met by a growl; Pieter was keeping his distance from them both. Louise too walked as if on eggs. What was wrong? When she glanced through the open sketchbook that lay beside the canvas, the crowded sketches tumbled over each other like sparkling wavelets rushing to the shore, but the face that stared from the canvas was as lifeless as a leaden sea. She wanted to ask Pieter, but he was aloof these days and tended to disappear into the far reaches of the studio, where she could hear him breaking things.

One hot, sultry morning, the storm broke.

'You're late!' Louise was taken aback. The Master had not asked her to be there at any particular time. In fact she'd been late on purpose; she was getting tired of both of these men and their moods. The canvas was on the easel today and the Master was pacing, doing about-turns that set his painter's smock swinging. He waved her towards her chair. 'Sit, sit!' he said as if talking to a dog. Louise was cautious.

He wasn't clowning; this mood was dangerous. There were livid spots on his cheeks that reminded her of her mother, but his colour was from suppressed fury. 'Pieter ...' he yelled, 'maulstick!' Pieter had it ready, but the Master still snatched it from his hand. Louise edged around them. Pieter looked pale and tight-lipped.

'Do you know what that imbecile apprentice says?' snapped the Master, doing a cruel imitation of Pieter's flapping hands. 'He says that you are dead. Do you *look* dead?' He waved towards the canvas. 'Pah! I am finished with him. Today I will tear up his indentures.' He turned on the boy, 'I can do it, you know. But,' he went on sarcastically, 'seeing as you know better than your betters, I want your *opinion*. Now, Pieter Kunst, perhaps you will gratify your master by telling him what colour he should use for the shadows that you claim *will bring Miss Eeden back to life*.' He hissed like a snake, and Louise backed towards her chair, looking nervously at Pieter. What was going on?

'There are some that would use brown, Master.' Pieter's face was white but he was staring the Master down. Louise wondered what would she do if the old man went for him – she remembered that he had attacked Pieter once before, over the painting of the wine glass.

'Brown!' the Master's scorn was palpable. 'And who said I would do as other people?'

'I did not, Master, but I am not going to tell you what I think you should do, because then you will refuse to do it out of sheer obstinacy.' Pieter's mouth was set like a razor; she realised that this fight had been going on for some time.

'Listen to him!' the Master was shouting, turning to her for support.

But Louise was not going to take sides. You don't walk between fighting dogs. She abandoned them to their argument. She only had one role in all this, and only one weapon. She thought back to her first day in the studio when this same little man had been provoking her, goading her with his astronomical nonsense. She remembered taunting him, and her moment of triumph. She leaned forward, and smiled at the memory. At that second she felt the remembered pose click into place. She had found the password – if only they would notice. She could hear Pieter arguing and the Master's sarcastic whine. At last Pieter's voice sliced across that of the Master.

'Look!' he said, 'look at Louise.' The effect on the studio was instant. Silence descended, sudden, but charged. She could hear the *froo froo* of 'our friend' on the windowsill. She heard the Master's sharp intake of breath. Their eyes seemed to be burning her face. She tried to think of Pieter – she was doing this for him – but she dared not look. It was now or never. There was a spot of red paint on the back of the easel; she stared at that. Pieter and the Master were mere hazy images floating around the edges of her vision. She sensed, rather than saw, when the Master took his palette from Pieter's hands. All their movements were slowed for her by the sheer energy that she was pushing out through her.

She heard the Master whisper: 'Blue, Pieter, go ... go get blue. You'll have to make it up out of the lapis you ruined the day she came.' When she heard Pieter respond: 'It's here Master, it's made up already,' she wanted to laugh, or perhaps cry.

'The way to build her shadows is to use her natural skin tints and then to darken them slightly with blue. Did you know, Pieter, that the blue of the sky can filter into shadows? Now, where are those damned paints?'

'Here, ready.' The children had stopped fighting, and Louise could feel her energy flowing out and into them, feeding their needs.

The Master's quiet voice called for oil. Now the pace was changing.

'Not that brush, Pieter … no no, wider Pieter, wider. Look, now I am the Master again. Remember how it was when the Begijnhof beggar began to sing his song. In a hundred years from now he and this girl will live … Dear God, I need more time, just a little more time.' He was bent to the canvas, and Louise could almost feel his brushstrokes on her face. Then, at last he dropped his head and whispered, 'Look, Pieter, she lives. Pieter, she lives!'

Pieter, watching over his shoulder, looked, and heard a fanfare of angels. But somewhere inside him there was also a tremor of dread.

Louise stood up, still stiff from her pose, and then looked at the canvas. She didn't like what she saw. She knew she wasn't pretty, but she hadn't expected to find her own face disturbing. There were unexpected echoes of her mother – not Mother as she was now – but the mother that Louise remembered challenging the wind when she was little. And did she really come across as so argumentative? *You are a demanding child,* her mother would complain. She smiled. The Master, sitting in an exhausted heap, patted her hand.

'At least she makes you smile.' For the first time Louise saw the picture, not as herself, but as an outsider would, and was a little shocked.

The following day, Louise tapped on the door of the studio, to find that they had moved an ancient suit of mediaeval armour into the centre of the room. Pieter was busy polishing it. She was a little jealous. It hadn't occurred to her that, now that the Master was happy about her portrait, he could be starting on another one. She looked around and asked where the Master was. Suddenly the armour broke loose and started clanking towards her while a sepulchral voice boomed out from inside.

'Squire, my horse! For we must
Pluck this damsel from the clay;
And let fair Hesperus,
Define her course.'

Louise had no time to untangle his riddle. All she could do was swoon into his arms, thinking that it was more like a collapse into a pile of saucepans than an armorial embrace.

It took Pieter and her a considerable time, and quite a lot of laughter, to extricate the Master, pink and triumphant, from his armour. It was a long time before she had reason to remember his courtly words.

Fabritius

Chapter 11

Work on the painting was almost continuous now. When the Master was not engaged on Louise's dress, Pieter was labouring on the tiles and on the background of the picture. To begin with, Louise sat for long hours, her hair carefully arranged by Kathenka, her dress billowing about her. After working on the silk for a while, the Master began to complain that the folds changed too much between sittings. After some serious rummaging at the back of the studio, he returned, doing a gavotte with a wickerwork manikin. With Kathenka's help, they successfully dressed this in the green silk and persuaded it to adopt a proper pose. Now Louise had to live with herself as a headless effigy while the Master laboriously built up the blue foundation, layer by layer, for the later yellow.

'Look at it, Miss Louise;' he would beckon her over, and make her bend to his view. 'See how it lies, a thousand dimples curving into every fold. It must seem to move to the eye, a living emerald, the most precious of all the stones.'

Louise made herself busy; an apprentice's apprentice, she called herself. She ground and mixed and cleaned brushes and palettes. Kathenka would come up with a tray and they would picnic together in the studio. Kathenka made cordials out of elderflowers and fruits as they came into season. It was a change from the small-ale they drank in winter. There was always a bowl of fruit and a basin of water to wash their hands, as many of the paints and powders seemed to contain deadly poisons: lead, arsenic, and mercury. After lunch, the Master would retire for a snooze, but Pieter would work on, and Louise would watch. If she became bored she would explore the far end of the studio. It was like an Aladdin's cave, stacked high with the curios that Jacob Haitink had collected over the years. There were elephant tusks, and huge shells from tropical seas. There were piles of books and open portfolios of prints and etchings; strange creatures floated limply in bottles. There were swords hanging on nails, and the suit of medieval armour, now empty, hung its head despondently.

'Where does he get all these things, and what does he want with them?' she asked Pieter.

'I don't really know,' he replied. 'He says that they are useful as props in his paintings, like the globe that we dug out for you, but it's actually that he can't resist anything new and curious. Half the time when he should be painting, he's poking about down here.'

One day when she came up to the studio, carrying the tray for Kathenka, she noticed that Pieter was grinning to himself. She waited till the Master and Kathenka had retired before she questioned him.

'The Master's given me the Turkey carpet!' he explained.

'Really? What do you want a carpet for?'

'No, Miss Louise ...' sometimes he still called her that, 'I am to *paint* it! Look at it – what detail – what combinations of colours: blue, red, green. It should be all wrong, but it pulses. That red is a challenge in itself. The Master says cinnabar red, but we don't have any. He says that Master Fabritius has a recipe, and that I should ask him for it, but I'm not sure if he'll be happy to give it to me – as an apprentice I mean.'

'Oh yes, he will,' said Louise confidently, 'He's a neighbour of ours. I will shame him into giving it to you. Annie doesn't approve of him, but he has always been polite to me.'

'Why does Miss Annie not approve?'

'Because,' said Louise matter of factly, 'he has hair on his chest.'

'He has what!' Pieter exclaimed.

'Hair ... on his chest.'

'But how does Miss Annie, your respectable nurse, come to know this shocking detail?' Suddenly Louise saw the funny side of what she'd said. Her Annie, with some dreadful skeleton in her cupboard, she hadn't thought of that. Pieter was looking at her in amused horror. She began to explain, but could feel a bubble of laughter rising inside her.

'He painted a portrait of himself. Father borrowed it when he was thinking of having my portrait done. In it his shirt is open, and his chest is ...' The bubble was dangerously near the surface now. 'Annie saw the portrait and was scandalised. Either it goes, or I go, she said.' For a split second Louise thought that Pieter was scandalised, too. Then, with a bray like a donkey, Pieter put his head back and laughed till the tears flowed. It was the most infectious laugh Louise had ever heard, so it was some time before they felt able to venture downstairs.

Louise still felt sore from laughing as they stood in the street outside the house of master painter Fabritius. She dared not look at Pieter, who was still fighting back suppressed little brays. He knocked, and then stepped back, leaving Louise to make the introduction. The door was opened by the artist himself.

'Miss Eeden?' he said with interest, recognising a neighbour. Then his eyes moved to Pieter, standing behind her. Louise began her introduction.

'Master, this is Pieter Kunst … apprentice to Master Haitink. He –'

'Oh, I know of Mr Kunst.' He smiled. 'Pleased to meet you, Pieter, I have heard well of you, and seen some of your work … perhaps more than Master Haitink would admit to.' He chuckled. Louise stepped back, and while Pieter explained his needs, she took the opportunity to examine the famous artist on the step above them. Up to now she had only seen him on formal occasions. They had interrupted him at his work. He had on a painter's gown, similar to the Master's, though it looked better on him. His shoulder-length hair was unkempt and his shirt hung open. With some difficulty, she kept her eyes away from his chest and looked at his face. He had a full mouth, set over a strong jaw. Thought-lines crossed his forehead. He must have felt her eyes on him because he looked straight at her; she felt the artist's quick appraising glance and his eyes kept coming back to her while he talked to Pieter. There was something animal, exciting and not unpleasing in his stare. Suddenly she realised that he was talking to her. 'You must excuse me, I was working, but the light is gone now. Come in and I will give Mr Kunst the recipe he needs.'

She followed him into the house. The parlour door was open, and Louise wondered if she should stay there, but he seemed to expect her to follow. They passed down a passage and into an artist's studio in the return at the back of the house. Louise walked discreetly about the studio, looking at, but not touching, the now familiar objects. On an easel was a painting of a goldfinch. Louise was entranced; the paintwork was smudgy but this in itself seemed to bring the little bird to life. She gazed at it for a long time. Pieter and the painter were deep in conversation. She wanted to listen, they were talking of quicksilver and sulphur, but she decided it would be tactful to leave them alone.

An open door led into a small brick-paved courtyard at the back of the house. Evening light filled the yard and with it came the liquid trill and twitter as some small bird celebrated evening. Louise stepped cautiously into the courtyard; the song stopped in mid-bar. She looked around but saw nothing. Then a sharp tweet drew her eye up to where a small but indignant bird, head on one side, challenged her from its perch high on the whitewashed wall. It was the goldfinch, the subject of the portrait on the easel, a slender

chain attached it to its perch. She pursed her mouth to whistle at it. Annie did not approve of her whistling; neither did
the bird.

'Tweet!' it demanded, fixing her with an eye as black as a
bead of jet. She pursed her mouth to whistle again. 'Tweet!'

'I beg your pardon,' Louise said curtsying, realising that
this was not a proper form of address. 'I'm Louise Eeden, I
should have introduced myself.' The little bird considered
her, as if wondering if her apology was sufficient. He settled
for haughty disdain. His face was scarlet, and when he
turned, there was a bar of brilliant gold down each wing.
She'd seen goldfinches before, but just in twittering flocks
that blew through the garden like the thistledown they fed
on. He began to work, bending down to lift the chain with
his beak. He secured it with a claw while he lifted another
section. When he reached the ring at the end of the chain,
he dropped it in disgust. Louise felt a hand on her shoulder.

'He did that for you, Miss Eeden – a sign of respect.'
Louise did not turn around. 'When he is in my studio he
has a little bucket that he can lower into his water supply
when he is thirsty. He draws the bucket up like that. He
would have offered you a drink.'

'I wish he'd sing again.'

'Oh, he will, but in his own good time.'

Louise, feeling just a little disturbed by the hand on her
shoulder, turned to go in. 'I love his portrait,' she said.

'I'd give it to you, but alas, it has been sold. The captain
of the watch bought it.' The artist bowed gallantly and followed Louise inside.

Pieter had just finished transcribing the recipe. 'I should melt the sulphur and quicksilver together first, you say?' he asked.

'Yes. And remember to crush it before firing it.'

'It sounds like alchemy to me,' said Louise. 'I hope I may watch.' The older artist chuckled. He spoke to Pieter, but looked at her. 'I am beginning to think, Pieter, that you may have found the philosopher's stone already. The question is – is it bespoke?'

As Louise made her way to the door she was only partly aware of the sound of Pieter knocking over a chair, and the painter's rich laugh as he stood above them on the step. Was it she who was bespoke? She had not thought of Reynier for weeks. Soon it would be autumn, time was running out, and she wasn't ready to be sacrificed. Not yet.

The door closed and they stood quietly for a moment, each absorbed in their own thoughts and their own confusions. Then, high over the house came the liquid trilling of the goldfinch from its perch in the yard.

'Listen, Pieter!' Louise said, and she took Pieter's arm and held it tight.

Louise stepped back from the window into the darkness of her bedroom to observe the two men. Their figures stood out like black paper silhouettes against the soft luminescence of the star-glow outside. Father, his beard as sharp as a scimitar, was watching as Pieter crouched, all elbows, gazing up into the telescope.

'Saturn…' she heard Pieter breathe in awe.

'You see how it appears to have arms out on each side?' Father asked.

'Yes … yes I do, I see them.' He gazed. Then he looked around, his nose knocking the telescope out of line. 'Louise! Oh, excuse me … Miss Eeden. You remember my empty glass? How I drew it with a halo? These arms of Saturn, they look like my halo, only it has dropped down over the planet's eyes.' He chuckled and turned back. 'Oh, excuse me sir, I seem to have lost it.'

'Don't worry, I'll find it again.' Father crouched gracefully while Pieter scrambled away like a spider. Father swept the sky, murmuring, 'Where are you now, old man … where… Got you!' Silence, then Father chuckled. 'Well, well! You could be right, my boy. You could just be right. We will write a paper together: *New evidence of a Slipped Halo about the head of Saturn.*' That would set them arguing, eh? *Evidence of pre-Christian sanctity.*' On second thoughts, we had better not mention a halo or someone will burn us at the stake.' He scratched his head, 'Why do we always have to end up fighting over religion? Catholic versus dissenter, dissenter versus freethinker. What are religions other than creation stories? I love a good story, but out there, Pieter, where we are looking now, that really is the truth.'

Louise sat on the floor, her skirts tucked about her knees, and watched their contrasting profiles as Father held forth and Pieter listened. The telescope, forgotten for the moment, pointed to heaven. This was familiar territory for her; they were absorbed, as she and Father had so often been absorbed. Now she was the observer, the third point in their triangle. Father was telling Pieter about his visit to Baruch Spinoza, the lens grinder, with his strange and beautiful philosophy. How could anybody long for heaven, Louise wondered, when it was all here, a universe to see and a newer, wider world to discover? When just to hold a flower or clasp a hand, was to gentle the hand of God. Who was it had spoken of the music of the orbs? Poor old Aristotle, surely. Tonight the stars were singing for her. She wanted to hold on to this moment forever. The night watchman passed, calling out that all was well, and Pieter stirred.

'I must ask you to excuse me, sir. I have told the mistress that I will be in tonight. You see, I am also the night watchman; she won't sleep easy till I return.'

'Of course, of course, but you must come again. Louise has told me some of your ideas about the artist's eye – fascinating. I would like to hear more.' They were all struggling to their feet. 'I must ask you to be as quiet as possible, my wife is … is not well.' Then Father whispered as he moved across the room. 'Next time it will be Jupiter, you have yet to see his moons.'

He opened the door on to the landing, where a night-light glowed. Pieter went out and started to tiptoe down the stairs. Father turned to Louise and held out his hands to her. She could feel his eyes searching her face, questing in the pale lamp-glow. There was no way that she could conceal her delight at the success of their evening. He took her hands in his and said in a low whisper. 'Louise … are you sure?' She looked at him in startled wonder. Could he really fathom her thoughts? Know what she was feeling? All she could see was the dark glitter of his eyes. 'Reynier – you know what I mean?' She opened her mouth. He was asking her, she would have to reply. At that moment a manic scream of fury rang through the house.

'How dare you! Call the watch! I knew you were up there. Viper! Snake! Antichrist.' The words were punctuated by the sound of blows. Father leapt to the door.

'Annie!' he exclaimed. Louise could hear Pieter protesting in a low voice from the landing below. But Annie was on a rising crest, screaming of Sodom and Gomorrah. Louise heard Father's voice, deep and urgent, join with Pieter's.

'You too!' was Annie's rejoinder and there followed a resounding whack, though whether it fell on Pieter or Father, she could not tell. At last she managed to move. The scene on the landing resembled a street fight. Annie, in night attire, had the two men at bay. Above her head swung the walking stick that she used when she wanted to appear frail. Both men were trying to protect themselves from the blows that she was aiming at them. Louise advanced cautiously, knowing that she would be the next target for Annie's rage. At that moment Mother's door opened, and there she stood in the doorway, a beautiful spectre momentarily restored to the woman she had once been. Her hair, tossed from restless sleep, seemed to Louise to be blowing in a wind remembered from their last walk together.

'Mother!' she whispered.

'Annie! Enough!' Mother commanded, and Annie stared at her, aghast. Her stick sank slowly to the floor. Mother turned with dignity, the door of her room closed behind her with a click.

In the stunned silence that followed, Louise steered Annie back into her room while the men retreated downstairs like chastised schoolboys.

'Hussy… harlot,' accused Annie as the steam of her indignation died away in short bursts. Gently but firmly, Louise helped her old nurse back into bed. But the sadness of disillusion settled over her as she did so. If Annie really had thought that Pieter was alone in her room, she had done nothing to protect her from his supposed evil ways. But Annie would never expose her to any real harm; therefore she *must* have known that Father was there too, looking after her. So why this outburst, why attack Father of all people? Whose interests was Annie protecting? Or was Annie the hand of God intervening at Louise's moment of weakness. And she *had* been weakening. In another minute she would have sacrificed Father's needs for her own. If Mother died, as surely she would, all Father would have would be his work. The potteries must merge. Mother must have the knowledge that his dreams would be fulfilled. The decision was hers, let this be her source of happiness.

Louise climbed wearily to her attic, closed the door, and pressed her back against it, blocking out the stolen joy of that evening. When she felt she had control of her feelings, she got ready for bed, moving stiffly, keeping herself in check, and fell into an uneasy sleep.

Louise woke with a scream on her lips.

She and Annie had gone to Hell. Annie was the guide,

like the pensioner who acted as a guide for visitors to the Prinsenhof and who took such relish in pointing out the bullet holes on the stairs, where Prince William the Silent had been shot.

'This is the Roman Catholic room,' she explained, as Louise put up an arm to shield her face from the heat of the furnace. 'With the Inquisition it has become most economical. As you see, there are equal numbers of devils and sinners so they can run the place themselves.' The scene was certainly crowded, but Louise was uneasy; a leering devil was watching her. He was part human, part beetle, and he held a bucket full of naked bodies. 'Sinners,' Annie whispered unnecessarily in her ear. From time to the devil would pick one up and throw it into the furnace, where it would sizzle and pop. Not surprisingly, the sinners were trying to escape, slipping and sliding over each other like frogs, trying desperately to get out of the bucket. She watched out of the corner of her eye while a woman slipped over the side of the bucket and ran for freedom. It was a futile attempt; a fox-headed gentleman, who Louise hadn't noticed, neatly spiked her on a skewer, and ate her head.

'I want to go!' said Louise, turning away.

'But they do it to each other!' Annie sounded surprised. 'Look, the gentleman devil has a present for you.' Louise turned back. It was the beetle. He picked up the bucket of sinners and threw the whole wriggling mass into Louise's face.

Her scream and her dream died as she sat up, staring about the room in terror, wiping at her face with her sheet. It was an old dream. Years ago the family had gone for a trip to The Hague. Mother and Father had business with a lawyer there, so Annie had taken Louise to an old church that had once been Catholic. Louise had recently been challenging Annie's views; asking her what was really so wrong with the Catholics. After much muttering, the caretaker of the church agreed to let them into a room where statues, carvings and paintings that had been taken out of the church were stored.

'There, that's what the Catholics are really like,' Annie had whispered, pointing at a large painting. Later, when Louise questioned Father about the picture with the devils, beetles, naked sinners and fox-headed gentlemen in it, he had seemed unaccountably angry and asked her where she had seen it. All he would say was that it was a great piece of art by Hieronimus Bosch; he then went off to talk to Annie. Louise decided to call him *Horribilis Bosch*, and she also made up her mind that she would never, ever, have anything to do with Catholics. Now she sat shivering in bed, too numb and tired to wonder what had triggered that dream tonight. Was it something Annie had said? She looked over towards the window, where the telescope, on its tripod, still searched the sky where Saturn had been a few hours before. It had all been so wonderful then. Her eyes began to prick. She lay back and in a little time fell asleep, crying for what might have been. She dreamed again, this time it was a dream of star music, but she didn't remember it.

A day or two later, Louise noticed a packet on the hall table addressed to 'The Agent of Cornelis DeVries in Le Havre'. She presumed that this was from Father – part of his on-going negotiations with Reynier's father. But then she looked again. Surely that was Annie's hand?

Father had not asked her about Reynier since that night; perhaps he felt he had said enough. He had brought Louise up to think and speak for herself. But at breakfast he mentioned, as if in passing, that Reynier's ship was not expected until the end of October as it would be held in Le Havre for cargo.

'Cornelis says that Reynier has done a splendid job, by the way,' he added.

Job?, thought Louise indignantly, he wasn't doing a job, he was swanning about the Mediterranean, even if it was for the best of motives. But she couldn't help doing a quick calculation. She had six weeks. A lot could be packed into six weeks.

The Alchemists

Chapter 12 .

To Louise's surprise, Annie seemed to wash her hands of her after the outburst on the stairs. Perhaps Mother had had a quiet word with her. Whenever she was near, Annie would sniff, and when she and Father were together, the sniff included them both. Father and Louise exchanged glances like two truants. One day, when doing a message down by the potteries, Louise was surprised to see Annie, walking along close to the wall of the DeVries works, deeply bonneted, and leaning on her stick. It was only a momentary glimpse, and in a second she had disappeared. Where could she be going, and why was her manner so furtive?

A tinge of gold appeared in the trees overhanging the canals and the treetops danced as the first of the autumn gales swept in across the Low Countries. Kathenka took Louise's cloak from her and closed the door against the blast. There was a smell of burning when Louise entered the studio, but her attention was drawn to her portrait. It was nearly finished now. The startling blue of the lapis underlay on her dress was turning to a brilliant, translucent green. The Master had at last begun to apply his secret yellow. She watched for a while as he delicately laid it on, layer by layer. She regretted the loss of the pure jewelled blue, but as she watched him work, she could see all the dimpled subtleties of the green Chinese silk emerging.

'I can almost feel it,' she whispered as she stood beside him. 'I have never *felt* with my eyes before!' He looked up at her, his own eyes red from the taxing work. Then he took her hand and kissed the back of it.

'One day, three hundred years from now, more perhaps, people will see this canvas, and you and I, Louise, we will live again in the minds of others. And if, by some mischance, the painting is lost and we are both forgotten, what matter! We live now, and you and I have done something great together.' He straightened his back with difficulty. 'The light is poor today and I feel winter in my bones; a hot toddy calls me from Kathenka's kitchen. But before I go, just look at this.' He drew Louise down by the hand so that she was kneeling beside him. 'Look at the painting of that carpet. That is Pieter's work, you know. Beautiful ... beautiful, painterly work. One day I'll have to tell him how good he is, but not now. I have to keep him on his toes. He wants the secret of my yellow,' he chuckled. Louise kissed the old painter on his cheek, before helping him to his feet. He winked at her. Then he put his head back and yelled:

'I don't know what you are doing, Pieter. You have forgotten to order the lapis we need to finish Louise's dress; you haven't milked the white cow in weeks, and all your saints in heaven will not make cinnabar red for you without you doing some work.'

'There,' he said, 'that'll keep him sharp.' Louise helped him off with his gown. Pieter's answer came to them from the far end of the studio.

'I am ready for the cinnabar now, if Miss Louise wants to watch.'

She made her way down the studio, past the dejected knight, to the area behind the junk where the furnace was set up. Here, everything was spotless and ordered. There was a stone-topped table and swept flagstones on the floor. Pieter had his back to her and was tending a charcoal brazier on the stone bench. She could feel a warm glow from it. He heard her arrive, and said over his shoulder.

'I'm going to fire the cinnabar. Do you want to watch?'

'I wondered what was on fire when I came in,' Louise said, and Pieter shuddered.

'Don't even think about something going on fire. That's why I'm down here, well away from our paints. Just about everything in paint is flammable.' He blew a little of the ash from the surface of the charcoal in the brazier and revealed the glowing coals beneath. She moved up behind him, thinking of Father's descriptions of the alchemist's laboratories he had seen.

Pieter explained what he was doing. 'Fabritius told me to melt the sulphur and quicksilver together and then crush the cake. I've done that. Now we have to fire them together; it's really too hot for the glass, but I have to stir it.'

'If we were alchemists,' Louise suggested helpfully, 'we would add base-lead to the mixture and it would turn into gold. An incantation if you please, Mr Kunst.' Pieter smiled but he was preoccupied.

'I haven't done this before, and it's quite poisonous enough without your adding lead to it.' He put a lid on the beaker. 'You must stand back now because of the fumes.' She watched as he waved the glass beaker back and forth over the bed of charcoal so that the shock of sudden heat would not shatter the glass. She crept forward. As the beaker heated, steam and smoke began to swirl inside it. A wisp of red appeared.

'Look!' she whispered.

'Now, I must stir.' Pieter gently lowered the beaker on the coals. The wisps of red were combining and precipitating through the swirling vapour. He inserted a glass rod through a hole in the lid and began to stir.

'It is like the fires of hell,' Louise said.

'Don't tempt fortune, Miss Louise.' Pieter breathed. Perhaps he lost concentration, but at that moment there was a sharp snap, the beaker broke and a wedge of glass fell from its side. A cloud of red vapour, heavy with mercury, poured towards them. Louise stared at it, unable to move. Then she felt herself being lifted up and carried away out of danger. The viscous vapour cascaded over the edge of the bench and on to the flagstones, where it spread, lost momentum, and sank, settling as a red carpet on the floor. Pieter's arms were tight around her, crushing her. But she didn't mind.

'Did you breathe any of it, are you all right?' he asked anxiously.

'No, I'm fine. If I did, you have squeezed it all out of me,' she laughed. He let go of her hurriedly then, and lifted the beaker off the heat. 'Can we save it?' she asked as he shook his head over the broken beaker. She bent down and poked the flagstones. 'Look, it's a powder,' she said. 'Come on, we can gather it up.'

Using old paintbrushes, they swept the powder into a pile and then onto pieces of parchment, finally funnelling it into a small jar. With what was left in the beaker, the jar was nearly full. Enough for twenty carpets, she was assured.

They walked back down the studio and found it empty.

'Where's the Master?' Pieter asked.

'He said the light was too bad.'

'The rogue. Look, the sun's out. I can't take my eyes off him for a moment. Now what should I do?'

'Milk the white cow,' she reminded him. 'Poor beast, not milked in weeks.' Louise was pleasantly aware of the pain in her ribs where Pieter had crushed her after the beaker had burst.

'Good idea.' Pieter agreed. 'Mistress Kathenka,' he called as they passed through the bar, 'Miss Louise and I are going to milk the white cow.'

'You can't take her there, it's a dung heap!'

'She says she wants to come. And it's near her home.'

'Take some more vinegar,' the Master's voice interjected from the kitchen, 'it's under the counter.' There was much clinking, and then Pieter found the flask. Louise took the flat flan dish he had been carrying and they walked out into the Markt Square.

'Where are we going?' she asked. 'Where do you graze this unfortunate cow of yours, and why the vinegar?'

'It's in the allotments, beyond your place. If you don't want to come, I can leave you at your door. The vinegar reacts with the lead.' The wind had dropped and the late sun glowed amber on the red bricks of the new houses.

'It's a lovely evening now,' Louise said, 'and if making white lead is as exciting as making cinnabar I wouldn't miss it for anything!'

It was a quiet time, early evening, with not many people about. They walked past Louise's house towards the allotments. At one stage Louise had a feeling of being watched, but when she looked back there was only one person in sight – a youth who seemed more interested in the clouds than in her. A grassy path led down beside a narrow irrigation canal.

'Have we time to sit for a moment?' Louise asked. They left the flask and dish in the long grass and walked to the water to where a single board-bridge crossed the ditch. There was a seat there and a rotten trellis held up by a mass of honeysuckle. In summertime the scent of the honeysuckle would have been overpowering. Now it was as thin and sweet as the slender song of the resident robin that had decided they needed entertainment. Autumn was breathing over them, a gentle reminder of the passage of time.

'So it's nearly finished?' she said sadly, almost to herself.

'The portrait?' Pieter asked.

So much more than the portrait, Louise thought, but she nodded.

'Do you like it?' she asked him. Pieter smiled, but he did not reply. Louise thought about all that had happened during this summer. 'I've loved watching you both painting, the whole science of the art, seeing how you work together; the preparation, and all the work. I had no idea how much work, but …' the word hung between them. 'But soon it will be over, won't it? The picture will be finished. Louise Eeden will become a moment in time then, captured and preserved like something in a bottle. I will be *The Girl in the Green Dress,* who seems to be about to say something, but never speaks, who seems to be about to get up, but never rises. Pieter, I'm no good at just being; I want to *do* things too. In the studio just now the Master said that in hundreds of years from now, we would live again through the portrait. You too; he thinks your work is wonderful, by the way. People will see your brushstrokes, but what about me?' She watched a small shoal of fish that hung and darted in the shallow water of the canal. She was sorry she had started on this; Pieter could never understand. Her impulse was to put her hand on his, but she kept it to herself and examined him instead. At first she thought he had forgotten all about her, but then she noticed that his eyes were half closed, and she remembered that first time on the walls, when he told her how he had drawn an empty glass. She smiled when he absently applied a stroke or two of paint to the air in front of him. 'Thinking?' she asked. He grinned, clasped a knee and turned to her.

'You've seen the Master when he's behaving like a bear, stamping and raging. Not many clients have seen that. Sometimes he bangs his head against the wall; sometimes he just sulks, but the worst time of all is when he has just finished a painting, particularly a good one. We're not at that stage yet, but it will come.' Pieter paused to think. 'It's as if there are two bears inside him: one bear knows it is time to stop, the other bear wants to add just that final brushstroke that the first bear knows will ruin the whole canvas. My job is to stop bear number two from spoiling everything. You remember the beggar?'

'Of course! I remember the beggar, and his picture, too.'

'I was inexperienced in those days. The picture was as you see it now, but the Master kept wanting to add things and change things. I realised that I had to stop him but I didn't know how. I was more frightened of him then than I am now. In the end I just said: "so the beggar is finished at last." Oh Miss Louise, it was as though I had got between his two fighting bears. He's shorter than I am but he grabbed me by the shoulders.

"Fool! *Pieter Kunst*, have I taught you nothing? You numbskull, you thick-headed bundle of skin and bone. Nothing!" He was shaking me as you would shake a sieve. "*No masterpiece —and this is a masterpiece – is ever finished.*" He turned to the picture; I could see that he had spotted something that he wanted to change.

"Master, please," I urged. "What do you mean by *never finished,* I don't understand?" That did the trick. He backed away from the painting, growling. Then he melted; you know the way he does. When he talked next it was as if he was talking to the picture.

"Look you ... you beggar. What are you, eh? Canvas, size, paint? You may be the work of the finest painter in

Delft," he bowed towards the painting. "But, turn you to the wall and you will be *nothing*. Do you hear me, Pieter? It is not you, or me, or Mr bloody Rembrandt – as he likes to call himself these days – that makes a work of art. No, it is the person who looks at it, the ignorant buyer, the wretched hoi polloi. It is the people who look on my canvas that make it a work of art." Now he was shouting again; "That's what *galls* me, Pieter. Don't you see? I've lost control; every damned person who looks at the old beggar will see him differently. It is *they* who will finish my picture – not you, not me, not the beggar; we will be dead and buried. That's why I hate to give him up, why I hate to see the old bastard go."

'We both stood there looking at the portrait. Then the Master began to scratch. "Which reminds me, Pieter, we must burn sulphur, to get rid of his fleas." Then he put his arm around my shoulder and said, "But there will be those, far down the river of time, perhaps, who will bring the old boy back to life for us. Who knows but that someone may even hear him sing."'

Louise wanted to put her arms around Pieter. She felt jealous of the Master, who was able to do what she couldn't. They were both so vulnerable, master and apprentice, giving so much and having to trust other people to finish their work. At that moment a sharp whistle rang out over the allotments. Pieter looked up, puzzled, and Louise noticed that the sun had dipped behind the houses to the west.

'We'd better be getting along,' Pieter said. 'I need light to milk the cow.'

The lush fertility of Heer Boerhaeve's allotment could be traced to an impressive pile of manure beside his tool shed. A texture like rich fruitcake was revealed where the gardener had cut into it. A wisp of vapour rose from the exposed face, a reminder to Louise that the evenings were getting cooler; time was running out. She shivered. A second whistle shrilled somewhere not far away. Pieter seemed nervous and kept glancing about him.

'I'll go and get it,' he said, climbing on to the pile, holding an old wooden spade that seemed to be reserved for manuring. He came back carrying a deep jar. 'This is our cow,' he said as he lifted the lid. Louise leant forward to see, and wrinkled her nose. Above the deep smell of dung wafted the astringent smell of vinegar.

'Why keep it in a dung heap?' she asked, as Pieter reached into the jar and drew out a coiled sheet of lead. A thin paste of pure white pigment was creeping from it. Louise hastily slipped the flan dish underneath to catch it.

'Mistress Kathenka can't stand the smell of vinegar, and the manure keeps it warm, winter or summer,' Pieter explained as he carefully scraped the coating of white lead from the surface of the sheet into the dish. 'That's it,' he said as he finished, 'the cow's milked.' As he straightened himself up, another whistle echoed through the allotments. A frown crossed Pieter's face. Quickly he thrust the coil of lead back into the jar and splashed some more vinegar on it. 'Let's get you home,' he said, as much to himself as to her.

They closed the gate and set off for the Doelen. Pieter took Louise by the arm and hurried her along, occasionally glancing over his shoulder. His anxiety was infectious; when a fourth whistle rang out Louise found herself copying him, but it was too dark to see clearly now. When they reached her door, she said, 'Safe home.'

'Close the door,' he said shortly, and hurried off into the failing light.

These were old terrors for Pieter. It was a relief to have Louise safe and out of the way. He remembered only too clearly from school how the older boys would pick on an unpopular child and harass him by whistling. The game was that the boy should never see or identify the whistler. Occasionally it ended in an attack. 'Pieter the puppet' had often been the target. He wasn't brave, and they knew it, so he had had his share of misery and bruises from this cruel sport. He walked rapidly; the canals and alleyways were black cracks in the night, full of menace. He should have brought a cover for the dish of white paint that seemed to glow like a full moon in his hands.

The first missile hit him between the shoulder blades with a soft thud. To his relief it wasn't a stone; dung perhaps. The whistles were closer now, shorter and sharper, aggressive little darts of sound. Another object hit him, on the shoulder this time. He hunched over the precious paint. There were whistles ahead of him, and a clot of something soft and wet struck him on the forehead and fell into the paint. He had no time to fish for it; he hid the dish in a doorway and started to run. The whistles were on all sides now, mocking, imitating the huntsman's call, 'away, away'. The next missile hit Pieter on the forehead and it was not soft; blood trickled down his face. Then they were all around him and jabs of pain burst out of the dark. He was a small boy again. He pitched forward onto his knees and wrapped his arms around his head, defending himself as best he could. Nothing was said – the blows did the talking. He could smell their sweat. They weren't tanners, or brewers either; both had their distinctive smells. Feet shuffled, there was the occasional grunt as the blows fell. Then came a low whistle from nearby. Immediately the beating stopped, and soft shod feet ran off into the distance. Slowly, cautiously, like a hedgehog unwinding from its ball, Pieter straightened up and parted his hands. He must retrieve the paint and get home. But he wasn't alone. His stomach tightened. Although there was no movement, he knew there was someone there; a mere thickening of the darkness above him. His scalp crawled. A draft of air that had found its way into the town via the Oosterport and up the canal wafted past the looming figure above him and blew gently across Pieter's face. He breathed in and sniffed. Was that scent? It was the merest whiff. He tried to place it. What did it remind him of? Where had he smelled it before? Then he remembered. Of course – The Hague – young bloods, disembarking from foreign parts, seeking to impress their sweethearts. Older men impressing their wives with the scent of travel. It was the smell of musk, and Pieter knew, as much by intuition as anything else, who was standing above him – Reynier DeVries. The fury of the bullied child boiled inside Pieter, and so he did just what his opponent expected him to do; he began to rise. All he wanted to do was to get his hands on his tormentor's neck and wring ...

'Oooof!' The kick went straight to Pieter's stomach; it had been aimed lower. The wind left his lungs and he rolled over, retching and gasping. The cobbles tilted and his hands tried to find a drunkard's grip on the world. Then he was sick.

When he came to, the stars winked clear in the sky, the menace was gone; so also was the scent of musk.

In the studio the following day Louise noticed Peter's bruises. At first, she accepted his explanation: he had cut his forehead and bruised his face when he had blundered into a tree the night before. But when he turned his back and she saw the round marks on his jerkin, she became suspicious.

'Pieter, what are the marks on your back?'

'Marks? Oh, I don't know ... nothing.' But Louise held him with one hand, while she rubbed the cloth between her fingers.

'That's clay,' she said. 'It's pottery clay... I know the feel.' She turned him around. Now she saw the bruising on his face in a different light. She noticed how he had difficulty in standing straight. 'Pieter ...' she demanded. 'What really happened last night? Were you attacked?'

'Oh, it was just the whistling game … like old times.' He shrugged unhappily. 'I seem to amuse them.' Louise stared at him and saw the pain that he was trying to conceal. Rage boiled inside her, rage that someone had dared to lay a finger on Pieter of all people. He was *hers*, even if she couldn't have him. Who were these petty people who had stooped to this? She felt like a lioness protecting her young; she wanted to roar. Instead she spun away from him and went to look out of the window. Her anger subsided slowly. Beatings were not uncommon in the town, but they were usually between rival gangs. Why would the pottery people pick on Pieter? Then a new thought occurred to her. Were the pottery apprentices setting themselves up as guardians of her virtue? She turned and confronted Pieter, her face flaming.

'Pieter, was it because of me?' He made a vague gesture that infuriated her further; if it was about her, then she had a right to know. 'Tell me!' she demanded. 'It's something to do with Reynier, isn't it?'

Pieter made no reply. He hung his head, avoiding eye contact.

'I tell you, Pieter, whether I am to marry Reynier, or not, is *my* business. No one has any right to appoint himself as my guardian or raise a hand against you or any friend on my account. Tell me. Reynier gets back at the end of the month, but I need the truth now. Did they mention my name to you, or say anything about Reynier?'

He looked at her then and she saw in his mouth a bitter twist she had never seen before.

'No, Miss Louise.' She didn't believe him, but she had to. He turned his back on her and walked stiffly away to the far end of the studio. She knew she was not to follow.

Pieter had kept his mouth closed, but he could not quite close his mind. Reynier was back, of that he was certain. Why hadn't he been in touch with Louise? For all that Kathenka said that they were not betrothed, it was obvious that they were destined for each other. Everyone knew that the potteries were about to merge, surely that implied that the inheritance was worked out? Pieter had known that this summer would have to end, that Louise would eventually go back to her own class and kind. He had been prepared for that, but he hadn't expected to be singled out as a rival. It was ludicrous: he, Pieter Kunst, a rival to Reynier DeVries! Surely his fate was to be just one of those faces that artists paint into the crowd about the Virgin, adoring, committed, but totally insignificant. Now it was as if the artist's brush had touched him, painting in that extra intensity of light and colour, that subtle shift of focus. Pieter Kunst was in the frame. He might ache all over, but if this was what his regard for Louise required, he would stand up, he would be counted. He smiled grimly at the slumped knight in his suit of armour and then set about painfully clearing up the mess from yesterday's accident with the cinnabar red.

Truth Will Out

Chapter 13

Pieter remained secluded at the back of the studio, and the Master was busily poking at a clot of clay that he had found in the white lead. Louise took the opportunity to slip away. She went down the steep stairs and through the Markt, following the route she had taken with Pieter that spring day when they had stood together on the walls. She halted on the high-arched little bridge behind the Nieuwe Kerk and watched the autumn leaves turning slowly in the still waters of the canal. The more she thought about it, the more certain she was that the attack on Pieter had to do with her, but why? She gazed at the floating leaves and something in the pattern they made prompted her memory. She was seeing, as if in the clear water below, a bonneted figure – Annie for sure – disappearing into an archway down among the potteries. What had Annie been doing there that day, and why? Today was Saturday. Annie went to visit friends on Saturday, so as not to desecrate the Sabbath with frivolities, but she'd be back for dinner. Louise would have to sit on her hands till then.

When dinner came, however, none of the family seemed inclined to conversation. Louise, Father, Annie, all were preoccupied with their thoughts. Mother's place at the table was vacant – as was usual now – and it drew their eyes like a lodestone, leaving them feeling empty, unable to rejoice or to mourn. Louise toyed with her food, waiting for Father to get up and leave her alone with Annie, but he did not go. In fact, it was Annie who was showing signs of leaving first. Louise gripped the edge of the table, her carefully prepared accusations suddenly deserting her, but she had to speak.

'Annie!' she said. 'The night before last Pieter Kunst was attacked on his way home. It was pottery apprentices that did it. I know because they pelted him with potter's clay.' Father looked up; he was curious, but Louise kept her eyes on Annie, whose mouth was pursing into a tight flower of self-righteousness. Annie knew something.

'Well, that wouldn't hurt him,' she said primly.

'No, Annie, but the fists and stones that followed did!'

'I never –' Annie sounded indignant. Louise was on to her in a flash.

'You never what?' She dared not take her eyes off her. 'I saw you down at DeVries's pottery with your stick and your bonnet. You were arranging something ... ?' She had her old nurse cornered. Annie might scheme, but she could never lie.

Annie's reaction took Louise completely by surprise. Suddenly the old woman's face went from white to scarlet. Her head began shaking like a turkey cock, trembling with indignation.

'But you are betrothed!'

'No, Annie,' Louise returned. 'I am *not* betrothed, nor am I engaged, nor am I promised to anyone. It may be my intention to marry Reynier DeVries, but engaged to him I am not!' She tried to speak calmly; she was now quite alarmed for Annie's health.

But Annie's reply showed no sign of weakness. 'You are taking advantage of the poor boy just because he is in foreign parts, and about his father's business, what's more.'

'Wrong again Annie! He went away because *I* was undecided at his proposal and *I* was unable to give him the answer he wanted. It was nothing to do with his father. He went to free *me* from the rumours that were sweeping the town. And now I want to know who started these rumours.'

'You … you hussy. You *are* promised to him. He told me so himself. He said I was to look after you while he was away. Oh shame on me, that I thought you were safe with Master Haitink. How was I to know that you would start consorting with that … that shambling half-wit.'

'*Stop!*' Father's voice slashed between them like a sabre. Louis winced and mentally stepped back. Andraes Eeden had been a notable swordsman in his youth but this was no practice blade that quivered between them now; his eyes spoke of sharpened steel and made a mockery of his smiling moustaches. Louise had never before been the subject of that look, and she did not like it. When he spoke again, her father's voice was icy.

'Annie is right, Louise. Cornelis DeVries, who is an honourable man, will confirm exactly what she has said. Reynier has informed him that you and he *are* engaged, that you have accepted him. You are his fiancée, Louise.'

In the silence of the room, Louise could hear the blood

hissing in her ears. She couldn't understand it. This was more than just a rumour. She dared to argue.

'But, Father, why has Reynier gone to Italy?'

'He went, as Annie has said, because he was sent. It was planned for months, albeit with some secrecy; he has been visiting the Majolica potteries in Florence. He will inherit the DeVries pottery in due course, he must therefore know the opposition, it is part of his apprenticeship.'

'Majolica potteries?' murmured Louise. 'So it was just a pretence that he was going away for my sake?'

'If that is what he said, it was not just a pretence, it was a lie!' Still the swordsman's eye was on her.

'But, Father, did you never wonder that he did not come to you to ask you for my hand?'

'I did indeed, but Cornelis told me that Reynier thought it best that your engagement should await his safe return. If something were to happen to him on his travels, you would not then be compromised.' Here Father stopped. He was looking at her, willing her to tell the truth, even if it would cut him to the bone. If she deviated one hair's breadth from the truth she would be cut down, lost in his esteem, probably forever. His voice was measured. 'Louise ... Daughter ... is it or is it not true that Reynier DeVries has asked you to marry him?'

This question was easy. 'It is true, Father,' she heard herself whisper.

On the other side of the table Annie emitted a little click of satisfaction. It sounded to Louise like a key being turned in a lock. She remained focused on her father. He seemed to be having difficulty with his voice for the next question, inevitable now.

'Louise, have you then accepted the proposal of Reynier DeVries?'

It was time for the lie. In one word she could realise Father's dreams and give Mother the comfort of knowing that she was married. This was what Reynier had gambled on, wasn't it? She could hear his voice, so reasonable in her ear, "...for your Father's sake ... his dream... your Mother..." All that was needed was for her to say 'yes'. But then she was hearing another voice – a woman's. "... if there's not something to be put right here I'm not Kathenka Haitink," and Louise whispered: 'No.' Then more strongly in case he had not heard, '*No.*'

For what seemed an age she could feel Father's eyes searching her, looking for any sign of weakness, any telltale cock of defiance that would betray a lie, but she didn't care now. She wasn't defiant, just numb. She realised that he was speaking to her then, softly as if to a grown child, but behind his words there was a terrible anger.

'Then you are the victim of a cruel deception, my child. Until I know the reason for this, you are to regard your engagement to Reynier as in abeyance. I forbid you to meet, or speak, or communicate with Reynier DeVries!'

She gazed at him in confusion. What was he talking about? How could she speak with Reynier, who was in the middle of the Mediterranean? She never wished to speak with Reynier again in her life. In a little while her heart would be singing; she was free. But didn't Father realise that it was he who was the loser in all this?

'But Father … the potteries, the business … your dream. Freedom to do the fine work you love… surely that's over. It was dependent on my marriage to Reynier, wasn't it? The loss isn't mine. It is not my dream that has gone, but yours.' She looked up, prepared to share his disappointment. What she saw both astonished and disturbed her. His face was working … Had it really meant so much to him? She should have lied. He began to speak but didn't finish. There was a crash as his chair fell over backwards and then he was on his feet and coming around the table to her. He took her shoulders.

'My dear Louise … do you mean?… But I think you do … that you were prepared to take Reynier for my sake? So that our potteries could merge and I'd be free?'

Louise struggled for an answer. 'I … I thought he was different – honourable at least. It seemed the only way to make everyone happy.' Her eyes blurred. She was past dissembling now; she had done her bit. She reached up for him like a little girl. 'Father, am I free now?'

His arms closed around her, just as Pieter's had that day when the beaker burst. As if from miles away she heard the door close as Annie left the room.

Louise fidgetted over her breakfast, moving the food around on her plate, but eating nothing. Why, oh why, did it have to be a Sunday, the one day when she had neither excuse nor reason to visit the studio? She had gone to sleep in a happy delirium, rehearsing what she would say to Pieter in the morning, but now her confidence was evaporating. Pieter meant everything to her, but did she mean anything to him? Why would she? She remembered, with despair, how he had reacted after their visit to the Begijnhof gate, when she had asked him if he liked her. He had frozen up as if she had trespassed on his life.

Sudden bursts of suppressed rage at Reynier would sweep over her, but these just left her feeling exhausted and unfulfilled. She wondered if she had a fever. She usually went to church in the Nieuwe Kerk, chiefly to please Annie, but she would not go today. Breakfast was nearly over, but Annie had not come down to join her and Father. If anyone had charges to answer, it was Annie. It *must* have been she who had spread Reynier's lies about their engagement. Had she really set the apprentices on poor Pieter?

As if Louise's thoughts had conjured her out of the air, the door opened and Annie stepped into the room. She was dressed for church: black taffeta dress and black apron, plain white cuffs, and a black skullcap with modest wings. She looked at the ground.

'Master, I wish to speak.' To Louise's certain knowledge Annie had never, ever, asked anyone for permission to speak; she just spoke her mind with puritanical directness. A moment before, she would have wished Annie to enter on her knees, now she was quite shocked.

'Louise, perhaps you would leave us for a moment,' Father said quietly.

But this was not what Annie had in mind.

'No, Master. Miss Louise should hear what I have to say.' Was there something in Annie's voice that suggested that her old nurse was not quite the penitent she appeared to be?

'Master ... Mistress Louise, I owe you an apology.' Her hands, which were clasped modestly across her front, seemed to be having a battle with each other; she bore on. 'I thought that Mr Reynier was an honourable man, but he wasn't.' Relieved of their penitential duty, her hands now took to their sides. She began to straighten up. 'Master, I felt the young mistress was in danger.'

'In danger?' Father asked. Annie kept her eyes down, but her voice had a righteous edge to it.

'Master, there are things on which we differ. Ever since the Mistress took sick I have felt the burden of the young Mistress's soul. Now ...'

'Her soul? So what great danger did you fear?'

'Not just fear, Master. I know!' Annie's head rose sharply with that defiant tilt that came from a lifetime of challenging people taller than herself. She fixed Father with a look that Louise knew, and it sent a frisson of apprehension through her. 'I speak of Mr Kunst. I have nothing against the young man's behaviour, and his looks are what God gave him. But there is one thing that makes him an unsuitable companion for Mistress Louise.'

'He must be the devil himself?' Father smiled, but Annie was having nothing of that.

'Worse!' she snapped, turning to Louise, trembling with emotion. But Louise was already in dread; she knew what was coming. That night when Annie had attacked Pieter on the stairs, one shouted word had stood out from the rest: *"Antichrist!"* Now Annie dropped her voice to a whisper. 'Mistress Louise, Pieter Kunst is a Catholic!' As she said this she made a small gesture, meant just to be dismissive, but which to Louise looked for all the world as if she were throwing a slop bucket of Hieronimus Bosch's tortured sinners at Louise's feet. Louise recoiled, but Annie was already moving towards the door, her black taffeta zipping angrily as she walked. Louise sank back in misery. She hardly noticed when Annie turned as she lifted the latch and said. 'Master, I have work to do, I will be late home from church.'

Louise was vaguely aware of Father making conciliatory noises beside her, but he didn't know the turmoil of her private horrors. He hadn't sat through Annie's graphic accounts of the tortures of the Spanish Inquisition, neither had he been on that furtive expedition to see that painting in The Hague. Louise would have sworn herself to be a liberal, root and branch, but Catholicism was different, even outside of her nightmares it evoked a mixture of terror and revulsion in her mind. Her nightmares were one thing, but she also knew that people really had been skinned alive, and roasted on gridirons, in the Catholic inquisition. Up to now, she had never associated these enormities with the quiet community of Catholics that lived here in her own town; her nightmares had always been of somewhere else. Of course … she must have realised that Pieter belonged to that shadowy community, hadn't she noticed the Master's teasing comments about 'his saints', but what did that matter? He was like Father's friend Baruch, the lens grinder, who was a Jew; he was different, that was all. But now Annie had changed all that. It was as if she had intentionally breached the dyke that held back the tide of prejudice she had been planting in Louise's mind over the years. Despite all rational thought, Louise could feel her natural inclinations being swept aside and drowned in a foul flood. As she pushed back her chair, she knew that Annie had found the one way to turn her from Pieter Kunst.

Father was gathering himself to speak, to say something *reasonable* no doubt, but Louise was in no mood for reason now. To hell with reason, she had to get out … do something reckless … prove to herself that she was her own woman.

In the hall she snatched a light cloak, slipped on her clogs, and stood on the front step of the house, at a loss which way to go. She would erase Pieter from her mind.

She set out at random, walking quickly, with her head down in case she should meet anyone she knew; let her feet decide. When she looked up and found herself staring into the depths of Heer Boerhaeve's manure heap, she wept. 'Damn Pieter, damn them all!' she sobbed. She cut through the allotments until she found the curve of the town wall beside the Schiekanaal. Little flashes of happiness and relief kept appearing at the distant edges of her consciousness, but they were just there to torment her. When her mind approached them they disappeared like the shimmering mirages that one sees on a summer road. At the steps she hitched up her cloak and skirt and climbed to the top of the wall. The purple cluster of toadflax was still in flower. She picked a sprig, thinking she'd throw it into the canal as a final act of rejection of all things past. But when she threw it, a surprise gust of wind blew it back in her face. She caught it and held it for a long moment in the palm of her hand, then slipped it into her pocket. She climbed down from the wall then; her step lighter and her mood somehow lifted. A glimmer of sunshine broke through the gloom, and, as if on cue, a clear liquid trill of song cascaded over the garden wall beside her. The first smile of the day spread across her face; surely that was her little friend the goldfinch? She waited, entranced, until it paused, wondering why its song should set her pulse racing. She was still smiling when the door of the house opened above her and Mr Fabritius, the artist, stood looking down.

'I hope it is me you are smiling for, Miss Eeden,' he said.

'Oh, I did not realise you could sing so high,' she answered pertly. Then, feeling that perhaps she had gone too far, she curtsied. The artist seemed amused.

'I am stricken; once more my little bird has outshone me. My wife has very uncomplimentary things to say about my singing. But, as to our tuneful friend, it is about time for him to come into his winter quarters. Perhaps you would like to help me?' Louise was hesitant. The invitation fitted her mood, but the man looked like his own brushwork: rough-hewn and gritty. A homely smell of cooking reassured her; his wife would be at home.

'If I really can be of assistance?'

'Of course. If he hasn't forgotten his trick he will perhaps draw some water for you in his little bucket.' She found herself mounting the steps.

The house seemed very quiet as they walked through towards the studio behind. She looked around for the picture of the goldfinch, but it was gone. On the easel was a part-finished portrait of a sea captain. Though still in the making, it was a strong face, full of life and vigour. She'd been right, his brushwork was rougher than Master Haitink's; it lived, but in a different way.

'Like it?' Mr Fabritius had turned. She could feel his eyes exploring her, and not just her face.

'Yes … very much,' she said, keeping her gaze on the picture. Her cloak had fallen open; she reached to wrap it around herself again. She looked up and their eyes locked. He was closer than she realised. She dropped her head but he read her mind and reached out to place his fingers under her chin.

'So, old Jacob Haitink has had the privilege of painting Louise Eeden.' She wanted to break away, but she was held by both hand and eye. How different he was from dear Master Haitink, who could touch her all over, adjusting her dress, pushing her this way and that without threat or intrusion. Her mouth was dry; she had to say something.

'Master … your goldfinch?' she whispered. For a moment his eyes flashed. Then he relaxed and laughed out loud.

'You are a young lady of character. Now we are neighbours we must get to know each other. Yes indeed, my goldfinch – Mr Midas I call him. He is outside, but should be brought in now. Shall we go? Then perhaps… a glass of wine?'

'I will let you go ahead, then it will be you that he turns into gold, and not me.' Louise was nervous, but excited too.

'Aha!' the painter laughed. 'So you know the story of King Midas, and how he turned his daughter into gold!'

Master Fabritius stood on a chair in the yard, talking and chirruping to the little bird while he detached the chain from its perch. That done, he handed the end of the chain to Louise. With the goldfinch perched on his little finger, he began to make a careful descent. Later Louise wondered if the chair had really wobbled on the uneven cobbles. However, in an instant, she found herself holding the painter in her arms, while the chair went skittering sideways across the cobbles. The little bird took off, filling the air between them with a whirr of wings. Louise felt a tug on the chain, then the pressure was gone, and the little bird was fluttering to the top of the wall, where it perched in startled freedom. She held up the broken chain. With a cry of anguish, the great artist suddenly lost all interest in her. He pushed her to one side and began calling and entreating the bird to come back.

'Quick girl, quick. Don't just stand there, get some seed. The jar on the window sill.' Louise found the jar and hurried back with a fistful of assorted seed and grain. The agitated master put some on his palm and began calling again, his hand raised. Out of habit, or good manners, Mr Midas bobbed to his invitation, but he seemed to be reluctant to try his wings. At that moment a rogue gust of wind swept over the top of the wall. It tossed Mr Midas like a jewel into the air, where he found his wings and flew to the gable of the house. Here he uttered a brief trill of freedom before disappearing over the rooftops. 'Look what you made me do! That bird means more to me than … than –' The artist stopped himself, his shoulders slumped, and he looked up at the vacant sky. 'I deserved to lose him, didn't I? Forgive me, Miss Louise.' He turned with a shrug and an apologetic smile.

She liked him penitent, but it was time for her to go. In that moment when only the beating of Mr Midas's wings had kept them apart, the last traces of Annie's spell were blown like a cobweb from her mind. What did she care about Catholic or heathen? Pieter was Pieter and he was *hers*. It was time to extricate herself from Mr Fabritius.

She put her hand in her pocket to get rid of the birdseed. There was the tiny sprig of toadflax, safe as a promise; she smiled. She was sorry he had lost his bird, but her mind was clear now and working rapidly on a plan.

'I'll look for Mr Midas,' she said, moving towards the door. 'If he doesn't come to me, I can at least tell you where he is.'

'You'd need an army of searchers to find him.'

'Just one, but we'll find him.' She smiled happily – mistress of the situation again, and ran for the door. She swept up her clogs and pulled the door open. There on the step stood Mrs Fabritius, her small daughter, and her maid, all having left church before the sermon. All Louise could do was to smile apologetically at them as, carried by her own momentum, she ran barefoot down the steps. She stooped to put on her clogs at the bottom and glanced up. The master painter was pointing urgently over the roofs. With a slight pang of remorse, Louise realised Master Fabritius was having more than the absence of Mr Midas to explain away.

Riot

Chapter 14

As Louise walked past the Nieuwe Kerk, she paused and heard the pastor's voice rise to a crescendo: 'Fifteenthly my brethren…' She laughed like the truant that she was and ran lightly across the cobbles to the door of the public house below the studio. It was closed; she hesitated. There was no Catholic church in Delft, so Pieter would surely be at home. Also, Mr Midas would not wait, so she took courage and knocked lightly. There was no answer, so she knocked more loudly. She heard Mistress Kathenka's voice through the door.

'We are not open for–'

'Mistress Kathenka, it's me, Louise.' Immediately the bolt was drawn and the mistress pulled her in.

'I lock the door when Pieter and the Master are out, and there was a rumour of trouble in town.'

'Oh, I am looking for Pieter,' Louise said. Kathenka cocked her head, as if wondering what to say.

'He's at church,' she said cautiously.

'But he can't be, there isn't a Catholic church in town,' Louise protested. Kathenka looked relieved.

'Ah, so you know he is a Catholic; I wondered about that.

Well, actually there is a church. It's tiny and it's hidden – the town fathers insist on that – it's down an alley off the Grensweg.' Louise was taken aback. The idea of a secret church ... a hidden coven... re-awoke the fears that Mr Midas had undone. For a second, in her imagination, the Grensweg seethed like a scene from Hieronimus Bosch. *Stop!* she told herself sternly. She must not start that again.

'Oh… I thought, I… I just didn't think.'

'Are you all right?

'Yes, thank you Kathenka, I just ran here too fast.' It was half the truth. She managed a smile. 'Perhaps you would tell me where to find it?'

Before Kathenka could answer, there was the sound of loud, unseemly shouting, followed by the clatter of running feet. The service in the Nieuwe Kerk must have finished. 'Apprentices, I think.' Kathenka observed. 'They are like young bucks; they get restless in the autumn. They will be gone in a moment.'

By the time Louise emerged, they had vanished. She pulled the hood of her cloak over her head and set off in the direction Kathenka had indicated. A group of three more apprentices ran past her, laughing among themselves. 'Fifteenthly my brethren …' was all she caught as they clattered away ahead of her.

She paused on the bridge at the entrance to the Grensweg, even less enthusiastic now than she had been. A canal ran down the centre of the street, with a path on each side. It was a shabby and poorly maintained part of town. A dead cat floated in the water beside her. Short flights of steps led up to the doors of the houses, showing that the district was liable to flooding. Halfway down the street she could see an alleyway on the left. From Kathenka's description, Louise guessed that the entrance to the secret church would be down there. 'The town fathers won't allow it to open onto the main street,' she had explained. People were milling about at the head of the alley. Perhaps the service was over and she wouldn't have to go near, but why were they all facing into the alley and not out of it?

She left the cat and moved down the path beside the canal. She recognised, at the back of the crowd, the three apprentices that had just passed her. If they had come from the service at the Nieuwe Kerk, what were they doing outside a Catholic church? She hesitated, she could hear loud voices raised from somewhere down the alley. There was a crash of breaking glass, and the crowd surged back, like schoolboys backing away after a prank. Louise realised that they were in fact all young apprentices, not a congregation at all. Keeping close to the wall of the house, she began to push through them towards the alley. A sharp whistle rang out, and to her alarm the crowd surged forward again, dragging her with it. When she turned to protest, she noticed that the boys had covered their faces with handkerchiefs. The whistle shrilled again. Where had she heard that sound before? Then she knew; it was the same whistle she had heard on the night when Pieter had been attacked. Surely this could have nothing to do with Pieter?

'Burn the Papists out! Down with the Pope! Antichrist! Free indulgences to hell,' the boys were chanting. Then one, his voice hardly broken, started shouting abuse that would have shamed even the devil in the Hieronimus Bosch painting. Their hate struck her like a gust of foul breath; she turned her face to the wall. How could anyone say such things? Then, in a humbling moment, Louise remembered how she too had been guilty of succumbing to her own mindless fears and prejudice. These were ordinary boys; someone must have incited them to this.

There was another surge; now Louise was being crushed against the wall. Seeing a window, she flattened herself against it. With her face pressed against the rippled glass, she could at least breathe. She had to get out of this crowd. Through the glass she could make out a box-bed, grey sheets spilling onto the floor, and a chair that was festooned with discarded garments. Sordid though it was, it looked to her a positive haven from the screaming mob at her back; the noise was rising to a crescendo. If only she could get in. The house stood at the corner of the alley, by looking diagonally across the room she could see, between tattered curtains, the rioters pushing down it towards some unseen focus beyond.

At that moment a door inside the room flew open and a rotund little man, soutane flying, burst in. Louise tapped furiously against the glass. He looked pop-eyed at the windows, then turned to flee, his weak mouth working. He shook his head helplessly and started backing towards the door. Louise was desperate; she tapped again, harder. He hesitated, bit his knuckle and then rushed at the window. No rescuer ever looked less valiant. He fumbled at the latch, obviously terrified at what he might let in. It yielded, and Louise tumbled headlong into the room. As he re-fastened the window, she struggled to her feet. No one in the mob outside had registered what had happened. The priest – it had to be the priest – stepped back and looked at Louise as if she were about to present him with the for-bidden apple. She spread her hands; she meant him no harm. A streak of egg yolk glistened in the stubble of his chin, and beads of sweat were coalescing and running down his forehead. His lower lip trembled as he spoke.

'I … I must go … I see there is no way out for *us* here. But you … *you* may stay; they will not hurt you … a Protestant.' How did he know? 'My apartment, madam … at your disposal.' He bowed apologetically and backed towards the door. 'I'm sorry,' he wiped the sweat from his eyes with his sleeve. 'You see, madam, I'm not brave … not brave at all, but my people need me.'

'On the contrary, I think you are very brave.' Louise cor-rected him gently. 'You saved me a crushing. But I must come with you; I believe I may be at least partly responsible for your troubles.' This was more than he could cope with. Bobbing his head, he backed into the doorjamb and then turned to lead the way.

'Perhaps we can escape by the roof,' she heard him mutter. With the opening of the door the noise of the riot burst in on them. Louise faltered. The room they were entering had probably once been the kitchen of the house, with a tradesman's entrance opening into the alleyway. This was the focus of the noise. Like all the doors, it was raised above flood level. A group of men stood at the top of the steps, their bodies braced against the door as it shuddered from the blows that were being rained against it from outside. A voice, startlingly loud, megaphoned through the broken glass of the window.

'Open up, you vermin. Send him out. If you don't give him to us we will burn you out and torch your filthy little church too.' The priest recoiled, stepping back onto Louise's foot.

'Who... who do you want?' he called, his voice shaking. 'Is it me?'

'*He* knows who he is. I call him the puppet. But perhaps he's too much of a coward to come out of his own accord. Tell him that I will cut his strings for him if he doesn't come now.'

They could hear the man's voice ordering away the people who had been hammering on the door. Then he turned back to the window: 'You can open up now.'

Louise knew that voice, and the knowledge paralysed her. Was she losing touch with reality? Reynier wasn't due back from abroad for weeks. She could see Pieter moving to the steps, but she was held fast by that voice, immobilised as a rabbit in a weasel's stare. Surely they weren't going to let Pieter go out on his own? They couldn't, Pieter was no fighter. It would be like giving a daddy longlegs to a cat; he'd be dismembered limb by limb. But he had already elbowed his way to the door and was now throwing his weight against the huge bolt that secured it. If she didn't move now he would be gone. She lunged blindly for the steps, feeling the priest's moist fingers slip down her hand as he tried to restrain her. Then the bolt was back and Pieter was out. She had no option. She threw herself forward, thrusting the men aside, and held onto his coat. Hands plucked ineffectually at her from behind, then the door closed behind them and she heard a clunk as the bolt was shot home; they were on their own.

At some stage extra outer doors must have been added for security. These were now folded out, creating a recess where she and Pieter stood. Standing behind him, as she was, she was almost completely concealed. She realised they must be on the platform at the top of the flood steps down into the alley. She could just see a protective metal balustrade. But why were they alone? Who had been hammering on the door?

Then Reynier called out, and Louise thought her heart would stop. He must be only inches away, hidden from her by the outer door. He was calming the crowd, speaking with that familiar ease and authority she knew so well, his voice rose clear above their clamour.

'Quiet, friends, quiet! We must be reasonable.'

Oh God, how she knew that voice and tone. She wanted to put her hands over her ears but dared not move. Before, she had been paralysed, now she was mesmerised. How or when Reynier had arrived she did not know... but he was here now, almost close enough to touch. There were jeers and laughter.

'Quiet, lads ... patience. Let *Mister Kunst* have his say.' She could hear the smile in his voice, all so relaxed, so natural. But she knew its deadly seductiveness. Hadn't she been under its spell since she was a mere child? How many times had she had to be 'reasonable' while young Reynier DeVries had imposed his own way on her childhood plans? How many times had Reynier got off scot-free while Louise had been punished? Then of course how many times had *kind* Reynier dried her tears? She had longed for his approval, but somehow the more he praised her, the less wonderful her small achievements had come to seem.

What would happen when he saw her? Her imagination made up the words for him. '*Come out Louise, old friend,*' it said. '*You know that we are made for each other; give yourself up. Betray Pieter, betray yourself. Marry me. There is no alternative …*' She found herself repeating, 'no alternative… no alternative.' The compulsion to come out from behind Pieter's back was getting stronger and stronger.

But it was Pieter who moved. It was hardly more than a twitch, a preparation for a lunge? But it was enough to break Reynier's hold on her. Louise's mind cleared and in that moment she saw Reynier's plan in all its detail. He was trying to provoke Pieter into an attack; that would be his signal. That's when the crowd would take over. He had already whipped it into a sectarian frenzy. But it would not be *Reynier* who would be implicated when they tore poor Pieter apart. No, Reynier would be gone long before they had finished. Then in a couple of weeks he would come home as planned, all innocent, to find the final obstacle to marrying Louise removed. She forced herself to listen to him.

He had dropped his voice; he was no longer addressing the crowd but was speaking to Pieter as if to an old friend. Louise knew that tone; the cat was about to pounce. Pieter must not be allowed to fall into the trap.

'You see, Pieter old friend,' he said. 'She may not have much in the way of brains, but she has the most fantastic fortune.' Despite her premonition, Pieter's spring caught Louise by surprise. She grabbed at his coat and threw herself sideways as he launched himself at Reynier. Fortunately this was enough. Pieter's co-ordination was never good, he staggered and he fell awkwardly, in a shamble of arms and legs, at Reynier's feet.

As Louise regained her balance she struggled to take in the scene. To her left, Reynier – masked – was leaning back against the rail that protected the top of the steps, laughing. Pieter was struggling on the ground in front of him. The apprentices, delighted at the sudden action, were yelling. She turned to face them. Now was the moment to turn the tide. For a second she felt like Joan of Arc; she raised her hands and shouted.

'I am not ... I never have been betrothed to Reynier DeVries,' she yelled. Her words were lost in the clamour of the mob. She might as well have poured oil on fire. The boys roared. Hadn't they seen her, just a second before, throw Pieter down at Reynier's feet? She was their new icon. If she wanted them to burn the church or lynch Pieter, they would do it. A flaming torch was being passed forward over the crowd. Louise gazed in horror. Reynier had started this. She turned on him; behind his mask he was shaking with laughter – laughter directed at her. 'Get Pieter Kunst!' he shouted. But Louise had only one thought: *Expose Reynier! Show him for the rat he is!* She threw herself at him and tore the mask from his face. But all he did was spread his arms and turn her fury into a passionate embrace. The mob cheered. Louise thrust herself back and turned. Resinous smoke from the torch blew across her eyes. Tears were streaming down her face. She could hear Reynier's mocking laugh behind her.

A sudden hush fell over the assembled apprentices. The moment of truth had come – and mob though they were – they sensed a point of no return. A tall apprentice stood in front of Louise, holding a blazing torch in his right hand. She stared at the lad. Why was he looking at her? What had she to do with all this? Gradually it dawned on her; he was waiting for her, awaiting her command. Should he, or should he not, apply the torch? The flame spat and crackled. She glanced down at the mob; most of them had dropped their masks. To look at they were just ordinary lads, but they were also a monster to be fed. The boy with the torch hadn't moved his eyes from her face. In a second she would shake her head; he would obey, lower his torch, and the church would be saved. But the monster still had to be satisfied; there would have to be some sacrifice – blood or flame – it didn't matter. Louise felt a movement at her side as Pieter got up. The sacrifice was going to be Pieter. They would take Pieter. She looked up at the boy with the torch, and shook her head; then she groped behind her for Pieter's hand.

Three distinct sounds cut the silence. The first was a woman's shout. The second was the sound of a blow. The third was a cry of pain. There was a shimmer of movement down at the mouth of the lane; everyone turned towards it. Annie's voice rose, shrill, indignant, and charged with the authority of age. In amazement, Louise watched her old nurse cut a swathe through the tightly packed mob, her stick rising and falling like a warrior's sword.

'Go easy, granny!' someone laughed as the crowd parted. She arrived at the foot of the steps and glared up at them.

'Annie, my old ally.' Reynier shouted. 'Up here ... up here, I have him safe for you.'

Annie bent to the steps, determination written all over her. For a second she stood panting, gathering her strength. She was coming for Pieter, Louise was certain of that; she drew him towards her. When Annie struck, it was with the speed of a snake. Louise screamed, but it was Reynier who took the blow; he fell, squealing in pain and amazement. There was a gasp of shock, or was it admiration, from the crowd below?

'You servant of Beelzebub! You have made a whore of truth. You lied to me about your betrothal, you lied to the mistress about the reasons for your travel, you lied to your father, and you lied to your fellow apprentices here.' Then she turned to the apprentices below. 'You are fools, all of you. You have let yourselves be led into a folly that would have seen you all jailed, if not hanged. This man is a liar and a cheat.'

'What about the Papists?' Someone shouted. 'Let's burn them out!'

'Leave them be. There are those that are damned in their ignorance, but theirs is nothing to the damnation of the chosen when they split their tongues with serpent lies.' There was a murmur, it might even have been of approval, but they had all come from a fifteen-part sermon and didn't want another. If they couldn't burn the church, they'd have to do *something*. Annie turned on Reynier, who was struggling to his feet, still groggy from her blow.

'You started this,' she accused. 'Now, you take them away!' Reynier nodded, but he was not looking at Annie; he steadied himself against the rail behind him. A trickle of blood ran down his face. It was Louise he was looking at. He addressed her now in a way he never had before.

'Louise,' he said simply: 'Will you come too?' There was no smile, no overlay of charm about his request, just a straight question, and Louise realised with a shock that this was probably the first time in his life that he had addressed her as an equal, as a human being. If he had asked her like this before … even once …

'No, Reynier,' she said, '… thank you.' What was the point of 'what ifs'? She had found herself an infinitely better man. Reynier turned to Pieter.

'So, Pieter Kunst, the puppet, becomes the puppeteer. Good luck.' He turned to Annie: 'Goodbye Annie. Of course it was you I really loved!' The old Reynier was back. In one graceful movement he vaulted the rail and dropped into the alley below. 'Come on, lads. Gone away… gone away.' His piercing whistle echoed off the walls and he was off down the narrow street, the rabble running ragged behind him. Whether he was the hare or the hound, no one could say.

'Perhaps he's not so bad after all,' Pieter said, watching them go.

'Don't add stupidity to your sins, boy. A leopard doesn't change its spots,' Annie corrected him sharply, before turning defensively as the door into the hidden church opened behind her.

The Hidden Church

Chapter 15

With a poorly concealed shudder, Annie refused Pieter's
invitation to take shelter in the church. So they saw her
safely off down the lane in the opposite direction to the
shouting apprentices. Louise hesitated, should she see
Annie home? Would she be welcome if she went back to
the church? Annie however was moving sturdily away from
them down the Grensweg beside the canal. Pieter took
Louise's hand; he'd never done that before on his own
initiative. With that, her mind was made up, she'd at least
thank the priest for letting her into his apartment. They
returned to the alley. The priest and some of his elders, if
elders was the right term, were waiting for them at the top
of the steps. He was wiping his hand vigorously on his
soutane, but when he saw their clasped hands he beamed
and put his hands behind his back. They climbed up the
steps. The kitchen was filled with the upturned faces of the
congregation: men, women, and children, curious but
smiling. Louise wondered if this was where they held their
services ... as in a meeting house, but then she saw that
there was a stairway leading up from the back of the
kitchen, where more people were gathered. As they walked

down the steps someone started clapping. A man patted Pieter on the back, a woman even embraced Louise. The priest made a little speech, thanking them, then addressing the whole congregation he said: 'Come, my children, let us ascend and there give thanks to Mary and all the saints for our deliverance today.' The congregation began to flow up the stairs, reminding Louise of a painting showing a mediaeval procession of the good rising to heaven. The thought was unfortunate, as it brought back to her the images of Hieronimus Bosch, and she realised she was holding poor Pieter's hand with a grip of steel. What if there really was some diabolical manifestation waiting for her up there? Perhaps the priest saw her confusion.

'Madam, please ... if you do not wish you to join us, there is my apartment ... at your service.' The prospect immediately dispelled any doubts Louise may have had.

'If I may sir, might I join you at your service,' she said, 'just to sit quietly at the back, of course.' She couldn't quite bring herself to call him 'Father,' and she knew 'service' wasn't the right word, but fortunately no one was in a mood to be critical. She was led upstairs, past the first floor, then the second floor. She had to abandon Pieter's reassuring hand, because the stairs were too narrow for them to mount together. The climb, however, gave her time to think. She had got over her resurgence of Horribilis Bosch; the congregation was just made up ordinary nice people like she met every day and, for all his moist hands, the priest was clearly not hiding a tail beneath his soutane. But she had never been to a Catholic service; what if she was asked to commit herself to something that she could not believe in? She hadn't managed to keep her mouth shut when the Master challenged her with Aristotle and his crystal spheres. Then she remembered Pieter and his empty glass. Perhaps there were ways of seeing the truth other than with pure logic. She would accept the challenge.

They had reached the landing on the third floor. The priest, with a word of apology, disappeared down a dark corridor. There was a plain board-door on their left; it had a peephole in it, but the door was open. Louise followed Pieter inside and then stopped in her tracks in sheer amazement.

'But it's beautiful!' she murmured, gazing about her, unable to disguise her surprise. Pieter was kneeling, and crossing himself. 'Genuflecting' Annie would say in disgust. Part of Louise's mind said *idolatry*, while the other part thought *but who wouldn't, in front of this?* She was captivated. The church was quite small. It was about the size of the Master's studio in area, but taller because the attic-level had been removed. All that remained now was a narrow gallery running down both sides of the room. Above this curved the beams of the roof. Looking down the length of the church, over the pews and the backs of the waiting worshippers, she could see the altar. Here there was an elaborate gold cross, flanked by candles, their flames stirring in the draught from the door. 'Gore and glitter,' was how Annie described Catholic altars, but this seemed just a natural part of the church. Dominating the wall behind it was a huge painting, its colours glowing in the dim light.

Louise was almost afraid to look. But there were no terrors
or torments here. She could make out a woman who was
being swept up into clouds – Mary, of course – supported
by a flight of winged cherubs. From above the frame,
picked out in a relief of white and gold plaster, God
reached down to clasp her outstretched hand.

Louise felt a gentle pressure behind her and realised that
she was expected to take a pew; she passed on the pressure
to Pieter. Let him go on, she wanted to be near the door,
where she could escape if she had to. She wasn't yet sure
how she would feel when the service began. There was an
empty pew right beside her, so she slipped into it gratefully.
After a moment, a small, gap-toothed boy climbed past her,
grinning, and disappeared into the space between the seat
and the backrest.

'Don't worry, Miss,' he said, looking back out. 'I blows
the organ, and it farts most terrible till I gets the pressure
up.' Louise smiled, and hoped that other people knew of
the organ's vagaries. She liked the feeling of being mixed
up in the mechanics of the church; it gave her a role other
than worship.

The Mass began and Louise let a feeling of detachment
separate her from what was going on around her. The organ was up to pressure, and a choir was singing from the
gallery above. To her surprise, the priest had a beautiful,
light, tenor voice. The congregation moved to the rhythms
of the Mass. At first it reminded her of a dance, but then she
decided the movements were more like a flock of birds, lift-
ing and settling and turning to commands that were clear to

them, but not to her. She had hardly recognised her friend the priest when he had emerged on the altar. She was grateful that his robes gave him the dignity he deserved. The moment of consecration came and went, and no devils danced in the aisles. An anxious-looking woman, returning from the altar to the pew in front of Louise, gave her an apologetic smile and Louise felt ashamed that she would once have thought of this woman as a cannibal. After the hate and trauma outside she half-closed her eyes and let herself relax. She felt as if she had walked through the frame of a picture. The individual parts of the scene began to break up and lose their identity. A phrase repeated itself in her mind: *fragments and facets of light*. Where had she heard that? Then she remembered Pieter's description of drawing his empty glass. But these were floating blobs of colour. In her dreamlike state she imagined herself in the studio; she should capture these colours before the Master gave her a biff on the head. Now the colours were beginning to coalesce. Was it a new vision, a new idea? It was so tantalising. She wanted to reach out for it, but then the blobs of colour began to find their places again, and she was back outside the picture, feeling as though she had been on the brink of some great discovery.

All the turmoil of the morning was falling away. What was all the fuss about? There were no demons here. Annie, dear Annie, so honest that she was prepared to take on a riot to preserve the truth that she valued above her most strongly held prejudices. If only Annie could be here, surely the music would thaw the icicles in her heart.

Perhaps it was reaction to the horrors of the morning, but waves of suppressed emotion began to sweep over her. She felt again the raw prejudices of the riot, so terrifying but now so trivial. She thought of the masked boy who had shouted such filth when she had been trapped against the wall. Why did people persecute each other over what they believed? All over the world they were burning and torturing – believers and unbelievers, Protestants and Catholics – all convinced that they and they alone had the true faith. Sadness rose inside her like water against a dyke, note upon note with the music, until it overflowed and fell as tears that splashed unheeded on her dress.

Louise was surprised at how quickly the ceremony came to an end. She hadn't even heard the sermon. But the organ was losing pressure, breaking wind again, and the gap-toothed youngster had appeared like a genie beside her. He looked up, and appraised her face closely. Then he shook his head wisely.

'Never mind me, Miss, they often sits back here to cry.' He clambered past her and made for the door. Louise pondered briefly about the people who came here to cry, then she too made for the stairs, grateful to have a chance to dry her eyes.

The congregation seemed reluctant to let her go. There was a feeling that she and Pieter, between them, had saved the church from being burned to the ground. Louise felt that they should instead be apologising for having been the cause of the riot, but what she really wanted to do was to be alone with Pieter. She had reached the bottom of the stairs first and looked back for him, but he was still caught up in the crowd. Now a new panic clutched at her. She thought back on the long summer and her growing affection for him. It had been so simple then; with Reynier standing between like an invisible barrier, neither of them had any reason to believe that they could ever be anything other than just friends. She blushed now at how foolish and unguarded she had been. She had got closer and closer to Pieter until she felt that all she had to do was reach out and he would be hers. It had never occurred to her that he might not want her as anything more than a friend. She remembered again the episode near the Begijnhof gate when he had withdrawn from her simple question, had frozen like the Schiekanaal in a hard frost. The memory was clawing at her.

She stood on tiptoe, searching for him in the crowded hallway, holding to her lips, as a desperate talisman, the hand he had so briefly held as they had come in from the riot. Then she saw him, obviously searching for her too, over the heads of the crowd. Their eyes met, his face broke into his broad shambling smile, and a flood of warm relief spread through her.

Mr Midas

Chapter 16

They emerged from the hidden church to leaden skies, but Louise had her own inner glow. In the distance the carillon on the Nieuwe Kirk finished on a single strike. Was it really just an hour after noon? So much had happened already today. They reached the Markt, both so absorbed in their own thoughts that their arrival took them by surprise. They had their duties, Pieter to help Kathenka, Louise to assist at home. But there was so much to say, so much to settle, Louise thought. They must meet again today; she couldn't bear the uncertainty any longer.

'Pieter … you remember Mr Midas?' He nodded. 'Well, I met Master Fabritius this morning,' Louise could feel the colour invading her face and hurried on. 'Mr Midas has escaped. I said I would look for him. Could you help me search?'

'I'm really very busy, you know.' Louise was taken aback, but Pieter could never dissemble long, and his laugh was already echoing through the square. He was teasing her. She wanted to hug him there and then. 'I'll see you here on the chime of four,' she said.

He was there for her as the last bell chimed, and they walked side by side through the Sunday streets. By instinct they followed the route to the town walls that they had so often taken that summer. Sometimes they were drawn together, at other times, as if by mutual assent, they walked apart. Louise told him how Annie had let slip that it was she who had asked the apprentices to deliver what was intended as a harmless warning to Pieter. She told him how Reynier had lied, not only to Annie, but also to his father, saying that he and Louise were secretly betrothed. The more Louise explained, the more she found she had to explain. Each layer of Reynier's deceit seemed to expose another. Even private things had to come out, like the fact that she had been prepared to accept Reynier so that the potteries could merge and Father could do the work he loved. As she talked, she began to see her behaviour as Pieter must have seen it and the demon's claws ran down her back again. A little rich girl flirting with him … using him to fill in the time until her wealthy fiancé got back from abroad. The thought that Reynier had waylaid her into deceiving Pieter, of all people, literally stopped her in her tracks. She turned.

'Pieter,' she said, choosing her words very carefully. 'If at any time I have shown you any marks of respect or affection, I want you to know that these have always been genuine and from my heart. I do not withdraw them now that I am free. I cannot withdraw them; they are yours forever, however you feel about me. If you want to walk away now, I won't try to stop you, but my affection goes with you … always.'

She faced him, trying to stop her lower lip from trembling. She had put everything on the line. Now it was up to him.

Pieter took his time in answering her, and when he did it was with the same formality, preceded by a smile, a bow, and a gesture that reminded her of Father.

'Miss Louise,' he said. 'I never have had any expectations. You must remember that I am just an apprentice without resources, while you are the heiress to a great fortune. Your friendship is all that I could ever look for, but that for me is a pearl of great price.'

She looked at him and thought: yes, they are alike, Father and he, not in looks but in understanding. She held out her hand and he took it, and they walked on towards the walls, side by side, newly vulnerable after their formal declarations to each other.

When they arrived at the now familiar steps, Louise knew better than to keep hold of Pieter's hand, they would both be safer on their own. Once up, she waited anxiously for him to arrive, looking out over the wall. The weather was clearing now, the sun shouldering its way through ragged rifts in the cloud. So much had happened since she had stormed from her house that morning. She felt in her pocket and extricated the little flower she had tried to throw into the canal in an act of rejection; it had become mixed up in Mr Fabritius's birdseed. This time however the canal accepted her offering and her thanks in a spatter of seed.

When Pieter arrived they looked out together over the exhausted fields where the lapwings tossed as they searched for grubs among the stubble. The wind was still cold and Louise wanted to move close to Pieter for shelter, but she felt suddenly shy. All summer Reynier had stood as a barrier between them. Now that he was gone, she felt suddenly exposed. Pieter seemed no better. Sentences came, and died stillborn; they found themselves mimicking each other's small but helpless gestures. The barrier between them had been replaced with a void. Pieter seemed to be even more tongue-tied than she, so it was up to her to break the silence. She remembered searching for a tune on her lute, absently running her fingers over the strings until some chance chord would spark the tune in her mind.

'Pieter?' she said over the fragile space that separated them. 'This morning while I sat in the back of your beautiful little church, I had a strange experience.'

'I hope it had nothing to do with Little Frans? I should have warned you.' She smiled.

'Oh no, Frans and I got on well. This was something different.' She looked out over the still landscape. No one worked in the fields on a Sunday: no horses, no carts, only the sails of the unattended water-pumps flickered as they lifted water from the fields, ultimately to pump it back into the sea whence it came. Pieter had his eyes half-closed and she guessed that he was preserving all this in his mind. It was a good sign. She would try another chord. 'Do you remember your empty glass?' she asked.

'How could I forget it?'

'While I sat in your church this morning, I had a vision.' Pieter's eyebrows shot up. 'No, don't look alarmed,' she smiled. 'I'm afraid it had nothing to do with saints, not even with Little Frans. But while I sat there at the back, I began to see the church, the building, the people, even the priest in his robes, as if it was all a painting. The colours were like the fragments of light on your empty glass – remember?' He was watching her closely now.

She hurried on. 'But I had a role because it was in my eyes that this picture was forming. Remember what the Master said, about how a picture is never finished, how it has to be recreated in the mind of the viewer?' Captivated by her new idea, she didn't notice the amusement in his smile. 'Religions are masterpieces, Pieter: stories, paintings, music, architecture – sacred all –' at last she faltered, because something strange seemed to be happening to the space between them. However he had done it, Pieter had crossed the divide. She heard her voice, far off, repeating, 'sacred all...' but it didn't seem to matter now. That was just the original chord. What mattered now was the new tune that seemed to be welling up inside them, and around them, over them. She could see her reflection in Pieter's eyes and wondered what he was seeing. But in her heart she knew; he was seeing everything that was Louise, from her wind-blown hair, to her heart's core, the good the bad, and ... but the new tune was filling her head and there was no time for thought. She could feel his arm in the small of her back, and her face tipped up towards him.

The last thing she saw before she closed her eyes was a flight of geese, flying high, in a perfect 'V' against the cold blue sky.

Their kiss lasted no longer than a long breath. Louise stepped back, startled. In a town where any public expression of affection was frowned upon, this was not the place to be; it was too public. She wanted to be alone with Pieter, but there was nowhere that they could go. She had to do something, so gathering her skirts about her, she set off down the steps. When she got to the bottom she turned to watch Pieter safely down. He was two or three steps from the bottom when he suddenly pointed to something over her shoulder.

'Look,' he said. 'Surely that's Mr Fabritius's little bird!'

'Mr Midas!' Louise exclaimed. She had forgotten all about him. She turned to look; it was a moment or two before she spotted him, sitting on a fence post. In turning, she missed the moment when Pieter walked off into space from three steps up. She got him to his feet, dusted him down, and they set off after the now startled Mr Midas like two schoolchildren.

They followed the little bird from house to house down the Oosterplantsden, the long straight road that bounds the town to the east. The high wall blocked off all view of the Schiekanaal and the country beyond. Streets opened at intervals on the right but the goldfinch ignored these, fluttering along the base of the wall, as if he sensed the freedom that lay beyond it. At the end the road swung to the right. A windmill stood on the wall here but its sails were idle, feathered for the day of rest. Just around the corner was the Oosterport, the east gate of the town. There was a water gate here where barges could turn off the Schiekanaal, and passing under an arch, enter into the town's system of canals. Road traffic had to cross a bridge and then pass through the arch of the Oosterport. If Mr Midas wanted to escape, this was the place he would do it, where he could see the fields of freedom beyond the arch. Just for the moment, however, he had developed an interest in his pursuers. Long years of captivity had made him a domestic little bird.

'Don't move,' Louise whispered, holding Pieter back. 'If he crosses the Schiekanaal we'll never see him again.' They assessed the situation. Ahead of them and to their left was the water gate where Mr Midas was sitting on the gutter watching them and waiting to see what they would do next. Beyond him was the Oosterport. Two black slated towers rose on each side; the pale brick of the arch was glowing in the late afternoon sunlight, which reflected off the windows of the rooms above the arch.

'I'll try to get past him and out onto the bridge beyond,' Louise said. 'Then if he sees me I may be able to turn him back. Perhaps he'll come down for you here. He seems to prefer men.' She sniffed, and gave Pieter some of Mr Fabritius's seed from her pocket. With one eye on Mr Midas she walked past the water gate, under the arch, and out on to the bridge. Relaxed conversation emerged from the guards in the guardroom as she passed. She turned; she could see the little bird now, a dot on the ground in front of Pieter. I knew he'd be good at this, she thought proudly. At that moment, the guardroom door flew open with a crash and, in a gale of laughter, two very tipsy members of the gate-watch reeled out into the road.

'Arrest that man!' one of them roared and then bellowed with laughter. Louise had to jump up to see over them. Pieter was pointing up towards the towers. She ran back onto the bridge and was just in time to see the little bird shoot over the high roof above the archway. Perhaps he was daunted by the unfamiliar sight of empty fields beyond the town, but he turned, fluttered back, and perched on the head of the statue that occupied the niche above the archway. Louise dared not move. She studied the statue: a watchman, complete with spear, lantern, horn, and dog. A tiny trickle of birdlime ran down his stone helmet. Mr Midas tried one more brief foray in her direction, then looped back and disappeared up into one of the sloping portals designed to take chains for a now defunct drawbridge. Louise tiptoed back to consult with Pieter.

'If we could get in there,' she urged, 'perhaps we could catch him inside.' The guardroom door had been left open by the departing revellers. They crept forward and listened. Resonant snores came from the room to the right of the door where the duty watchman was sleeping off his Sunday roast and a bellyful of ale. Carrying their Sunday shoes, they slipped in. Ahead of them rose a flight of stone stairs. They mounted, looking for a door that might open into the room above the archway. When they found it, it didn't look much used, but when Louise raised the latch and pushed, it opened easily enough. Light from a high dusty window filtered down on to them. There was no sign of Mr Midas but Louise thought she heard a tiny movement behind the crude shutters that had been propped up to block the portals, presumably to prevent jackdaws coming in to nest. She put down her shoes, crossed the room, and eased back the shutter. There below her was Mr Midas, head cocked, looking up at her with a single bright eye. Hardly daring to move, she trickled some seed down the slope, and then retreated, leaving, grain by grain, a trail of seed leading into the room. She beckoned Pieter in, signalling that he should close the door so that Mr Midas would not escape. There was nothing to do now but wait.

Henk Blut, gatekeeper at the Oosterport, woke with a start to the sound of bird-song. At first he thought that the sound was inside his head, a notion that was painfully dispelled when he shook it. Pain stabbed upwards from his neck and spread into his forehead. The song, however, persisted. Avoiding any further violent movement, he took up his musket and went to the door under the arch and peered up and down the road. No bird, and no song. When he turned back into the gatehouse, he distinctly heard the singing again. It appeared to be coming from upstairs. Still in his stockinged feet, he climbed the stone steps. That was strange, the singing seemed to come from the room over the archway. He raised the latch slowly and inched the door open. A nearly horizontal beam of sunlight shone in from the west, projecting a golden square onto the stone wall. There, perched on a rusty spike, was a goldfinch, head back, singing its heart out. A short length of chain hung from its leg. Henk, a keen sportsman, raised his musket. Then the thought of an explosion in that enclosed space made him wince, and he lowered the weapon. The chain intrigued him; perhaps the bird was worth money. He was broke, as usual. He peered into the dim room, looking for an owner. It was at that moment that he saw the young couple, locked in embrace, totally oblivious of him and of everything else in the world. He struggled valiantly with a weak sense of civic duty and with an even weaker puritanical heart. Another half-hour of sleep would see him right, he thought. He backed out of the room and pulled the door after him, sighing for his lost youth. Perhaps they, and the bird, would be gone when he woke up.

They walked home together in the darkening streets with Mr Midas perched contentedly on Pieter's finger. They said good night to Willy Claes outside the powder store. Louise remembered the time that she and Pieter had walked back past the powder store after their first visit to the town walls. Everything was all right now, even his illicit smoking seemed a harmless occupation.

As they approached Mr Fabritius's house Louise was having second thoughts about Mr Midas. It seemed a shame to return him to captivity. Also, for reasons she didn't want to have to explain to Pieter, she did not really want to knock on the Fabritius door. They decided to set him free where he could fly home if he wished. Pieter undid the chain in case it caught on something, and Mr Midas disappeared up into one of the great trees near the house.

The Lapis Arrives

Chapter 17

The lapis, that Pieter had eventually ordered, had arrived. He weighed the packet in his hand. It felt light; it had better be good quality, otherwise there would not be enough, and the Master would have yet another excuse for delay. Only a single panel of Louise's dress remained to be painted. The Master had already been growling, at once hating to finish it and yet wanting it to be done. Pieter cut the stitching on the cloth-bound packet and eased the inner wrappings apart. He sucked his breath through his teeth in appreciation. Surely this was gem quality material. He eased out a particularly beautiful flake and turned it in the light. He smiled in recollection; he had been grinding lapis that day when Louise had walked into their lives. What was it the Master had said all that time ago? *One day, Pieter, someone will walk into my studio who is without conceit.* He hadn't been defeated though; this was his finest work ever.

Pieter had visited Louise's house twice in the week following the riot, both times at Mr Eeden's invitation. The first time had been to report on the progress of Louise's portrait. He had started to apologise about the awaited lapis but Mr Eeden had just laughed and had begun questioning him about how they compounded their colours. Soon Pieter's stutter had vanished, and his hands did what they were told; he forgot that he was speaking to a Master of the Guild, and didn't notice Louise quietly smiling to herself.

At Pieter's suggestion, the congregation at the hidden church made no formal complaint about the riot or the damage that had been done to the church. An anonymous donation, however, more than compensated for the damage done. News soon reached the town that young Reynier DeVries was extending his studies abroad for an indefinite period; clearly the rumours about Miss Eeden's betrothal had been unfounded. If it caused mild surprise that the merger of the two potteries appeared to be going ahead without Miss Eeden's betrothal, the fact that the merger made business sense on its own was an adequate explanation.

Pieter turned the lapis in his hand and shook his head. He was reluctant to stop daydreaming. The stone was perfect, no crust of limestone to be laboriously chipped and scraped away. All he had to do was to drop it onto his grindstone and begin reducing it – carefully this time – to the precise grain size. As he began the laborious process he thought about a suggestion that Mr Eeden had made on his last visit. He had been invited to see the moons on Jupiter. It was long after curfew when he got ready to leave, so the only thing to do was to wait so that he could walk home with the watch. They were standing in the starlit doorway when Mr Eeden put his hand on Pieter's sleeve. Pieter remembered how he had so nearly drawn it away, embarrassed at how coarse the cheap cloth must feel to the gentleman.

'You know, Pieter. When the time comes, your subscription to the Guild of St Luke need not be a problem. A patron can help a young lad along, it is quite in order.' Before Pieter could mumble out his thanks he found that he was being pushed down the steps. 'Look, here's the watch. Off with you now. Goodnight.' It was typical. Mr Eeden had timed his offer for the arrival of the watch. All Pieter could do was mouth his thanks to the closing door.

Pieter looked up and blinked. The light in the studio had changed suddenly. The change had come and gone faster than any lightning flash. He looked at the window, and what he saw there was unbelievable. The leaded panes were curved into the room, as if a gigantic wind was blowing in on them from outside. Each square was haloed by a fine spray of coloured glass, where the panes were crackling along their edges. At the moment when it seemed that the windows must inevitably burst inwards, they were instantly sucked out and were gone. All this happened in perfect silence. Then, as the ceiling lifted above him, a roar, as of some demented animal, rose through the floor and slammed into him from every side. The clamour went on and on, and Pieter, who had instinctively thrown himself over his precious grinding, found that he was yelling at the top of his voice at the sheer outrage of it all.

When the din stopped, he gazed dumbly out through the

eyeless windows. Debris of every kind was plummeting out of the sky, screened by a curtain of falling tiles that slipped from the roof above. He looked about the studio foolishly; surely there was something he should be doing. Louise's portrait had been knocked skew-wise on its easel. He crossed the studio to right her and gazed in disbelief at the sprinkle of fine glass on the canvas. He began to blow it off.

Suddenly a dreadful constriction gripped his throat. The phenomenon, whatever it was, had happened so quickly, and so violently that he had no time to rationalise it. It had seemed meaningless. Now, as reason returned, it took on a meaning that was too dreadful even to contemplate. Pieter's body reacted instinctively, without any conscious instruction from his brain.

He half ran, half fell, down the stairs and rushed through the bar, where stunned customers still clutched their beer jugs. Outside he dodged the rain of debris by the Nieuwe Kerk, where the black slates skimmed like scimitars from the roof. He turned towards the Doelen, towards where Louise Eeden's house stood, and entered a nightmare out of hell. He was seeing light where no light should be. There was a rampart of debris ahead; he climbed it without realising what he was doing. He stood on its crest, trying to comprehend where he was. The town walls had been toppled. His eyes tracked down, drawn as if to the vanishing point of a picture. At the point of focus, in place of the powder house, a vast cavity reeked. It was fully fifteen feet deep.

Pieter was the first to see the shattered stumps of the great trees that had stood about the Doelen where Louise's thrush had sung. And he was the first to look out over the tormented sea of rubble where her home had been. Now his mind registered what his body had known since his precipitate flight down the stairs. Louise Eeden was dead.

A sympathetic member of the watch delivered a distraught Pieter back to Kathenka before returning to his grisly task.

Delft, 1667

Dirck van Vliet looked out over the new red tiles adorning the houses about the Markt. At last the town was beginning to look like itself again. His left hand made rhythmic sweeps over the untouched page before him. He was trying to think himself back to that day, thirteen years before, when eighty thousand pounds of gunpowder, held in the town's gunpowder magazine, had exploded, no one knew why. He had been Officer in Charge of the watch that day, and the time and date were engraved on his mind: half past ten in the morning, October 12th 1654. His ears, deaf before their time, still hissed from the blast he had received that day. How could he write about something so preposterous? But if he didn't, who would? And perhaps the words would ease his inner pain. He dipped his quill, and watched the wet ink follow the sweeping strokes of the pen across the page.

'The arch of heaven seemed to crack and to burst,
the whole earth to split, and hell open its jaws; in

consequence of which not only the town and the
whole land of Delft with all her lovely villages
shook and trembled, but the whole of Holland
rocked from the ghastly rumble. The sound was
heard as far as Den Helder, yes, on the island of
Texel, on the North Sea. We saw –'

He crossed that out and began the sentence again...

'They saw such a frightful mixture of smoke and
vapour rise, just as if the pools of hell had opened
their throats ... '

Tears slid unexpectedly down his cheeks; his eye was drawn yet
again to the list of casualties that he and his colleagues had com-
piled when their gruesome work in the ruins was done. So many
friends – so much talent. His finger searched down the column,
then stopped. Here was one: Master Painter Carel Fabritius, his
wife and servants. He looked up at the painting hanging above his
desk. The little goldfinch looked down on him from the canvas, as
fresh as the day it was painted. He smiled, remembering how the
little bird had sung on the day when he had bought the painting.
He turned back to the list with a sigh. There, a little higher up, was
another well-known name: Master Potter Andraes Eeden, his wife,
daughter, nursemaid, and servant.

He closed his eyes, trying to recall Andraes's face, but another
image came unbidden to his mind. He and the watch had just
emerged from the shooting range when they met Andraes's girl,
Louise, walking home with that lad from Haitink's studio. The
watch were a merry bunch in those days, and they had all accompanied the girl to her door. He remembered her as she had turned

on the steps of the house to say goodnight; that was all. Strange that her face, caught in that moment, should stay etched in his mind over all these years.

He picked up his pen.

ABOUT *WINGS OVER DELFT* ...

Although Louise Eeden, her family and Pieter are characters of my own creating, some of the people and events in the book are factual, and I have as far as possible tried to place her story in a credible historical and geographical setting.

The modern visitor to the little Dutch town of Delft will be able to see the Markt, and imagine looking down into it from the Master's studio. The Nieuwe Kerk has a new spire, but the tower of the Oude Kirke really does tilt as it did in Louise's day. One can see the Begijnhof gate – where the beggar sat – and look up at the stone watchman and his dog on the Oosterport where Mr Midas perched. Both no doubt have suffered from three and a half centuries of pottery fumes. The high walls that surrounded Delft in Louise's day have long since been dismantled, letting in both the light and the air that she craved.

Brewing was once the main industry in Delft. When this declined, the industrious inhabitants turned to pottery making, producing cups and jugs, plates and tiles painted in blue on white. Often the designs were local scenes – even today windmills decorate modern souvenirs. There were, however, artist-craftsmen who were copying Chinese designs of great beauty and delicacy. In the story, Louise's father wanted, above all, to spend time on this sort of work. All artists had to belong to the Guild of St Luke – the guild of artists and craftsmen – before they could sell their work or teach. In addition to potters, the Guild included tapestry and glass makers, booksellers, and of course, painters. Membership was not cheap. When Louise's father offered to help Pieter with the price of membership of the Guild, it was not only a token of approval, but an offer to advance his career.

This was a time of unprecedented artistic activity, not just in Delft, but in Holland as a whole. Wealth was pouring into the country from colonies in Indonesia and the Far East. One of the ways of dispersing one's wealth, and showing one's good taste, was to commission a work of art. A betrothal would provide an excuse for a portrait of one, or even both partners. In Amsterdam, Rembrandt was at the height of his artistic powers – even if his finances were shaky – but there were at least two artists in Delft that Mr Eeden could have chosen for Louise's portrait. One was the young Johannes Vermeer, who had just joined the Guild, and the other was Carel Fabritius, who features in the book as Mr Eeden's ruggedly handsome neighbour. There is a striking self-portrait of Fabritius in the Rijksmuseum in Amsterdam on which I have based my description of him. The suggestion that he had a roving eye is my own addition. Mr Midas, as I call his goldfinch, was real, and if you are ever in the Mauritshuis in The Hague, just a few miles west of Delft, you can see what he looked like from the portrait that Fabritius painted of him. Here it hangs almost side by side with Vermeer's famous 'View of Delft'.

There seems to be no doubt that Vermeer used a *camera obscura* to achieve his wonderful likenesses. Other artists, such as Rembrandt and Rubens, however, did not use optical aids. I felt that it was more in character for Master Haitink to work by eye rather than by using optics. As far as possible I have tried to be accurate when giving details of painting methods, and compounding colours.

Despite the strictures of Calvinism, the Dutch were tolerant both of other religions and of freethinkers. In many cities, Catholics were allowed to worship, provided they did so in secrecy. Carefully constructed hidden churches were built in attics. Access had to be down alleyways off the main thoroughfares. It is, however, almost certain that there was no hidden Catholic church in Delft in 1654. Vermeer, who converted to Catholicism on his marriage in 1653, had to go elsewhere for his conversion. The church that I made up for Delft is a scaled down version of the delightful little attic church, now the Amstelkring Museum in Amsterdam. This is open to the public, and you can see the priest's quarters as they were in the seventeenth century. Not far from this is Rembrandt's house, which also provided material, both for Louise's father's visit to the great artist, and to furnish Master Haitink's collection of curiosities at the back of his studio.

Just north from the Rembrandt House was the Jewish quarter where Louise's father went to visit Spinoza. Benedict Spinoza was to become one of the great philosophers of all time, but in 1654 he was quite young and making a living out of grinding lenses. (At the time of our story he was called Baruch, but later changed his name to Benedict.) By leaning on the fact that most ideas exist in the mind long before they can be put down on paper, I have anticipated ideas that would later form part of his philosophy. Spinoza died in 1677 aged only forty-four years; it is thought that the glass dust he had inhaled during his years as a lens grinder contributed to his early death.

The explosion known as the Delft Thunderclap is a historical fact. I have borrowed from Dirck van Bleyswijck's graphic account of the explosion, written in 1667, for my imaginary Dirck van Vliet to recall the event. I have also let him borrow Fabritius's painting of the goldfinch. The captain of the watch, being a gentleman, would be a likely purchaser of such a picture. Bleyswijck records that over 200 houses were destroyed in the explosion in which the 'huge strong trees in the Doelen were mostly chopped off level with the ground.' He gives no count of the casualties, but among those who died was Carel Fabritius, the artist who had so beautifully painted the little goldfinch. He was only thirty-two years of age.

I have used many sources to help me with the writing of *Wings Over Delft*. PTA Swillens, in *Johannes Vermeer, Painter of Delft 1632–1675*, gives a wealth of information on the local history and on the painting techniques of the time. *Vermeer*, by John Nash, published by the Rijksmuseum, Amsterdam, is a more recent account, and is beautifully illustrated. Anyone interested in the optical techniques used by Vermeer, and by other artists over the years, should read David Hockney's *Secret Knowledge*. In *Rembrandt's Eyes*, Simon Schama provided a model for the Master in his wonderfully perceptive description of Rembrandt's artistry. Norman Davies's *Europe, A History*, never leaves my desk.

Aubrey Flegg

TO COME ...

THE RAINBOW BRIDGE
Book 2: the *Louise* trilogy

France, 1792. Revolution is sweeping the country; King Louis has been deposed. Eighteen-year-old cadet Gaston Moreau leaves home to join the Hussars. Two years later, Gaston, now a Lieutenant, is hurrying to catch up with a French expeditionary force that is driving towards Amsterdam, when his column is halted. Fooled by his cadets into thinking that a lady is drowning in the canal, Gaston plunges into the icy water. What he rescues is not a flesh-and-blood woman, but the portrait of Louise Eeden ...

IN THE CLAWS OF THE EAGLE
Book 3: the *Louise* trilogy

Vienna, late nineteenth century. Little Isaac Abrahams is showing early signs of talent on the violin. He often practises to an audience of just one – the lady in the picture on the wall of his parents' house. After the Anschluss of 1939, Isaac, now a famous violin virtuoso, is taken to the Theresienstadt concentration camp, and thence to Auschwitz. The portrait of Louise falls into the hands of an SS officer named Heinrich, and seems destined to join the collection being stolen from the galleries and private collection of Europe on the express orders of Adolf Hitler ...

Other Books by Aubrey Flegg

KATIE'S WAR

Winner Peter Pan Award (IBBY Sweden)
When Katie's father returns from the Great
War, he is shell-shocked. Four years later
he has almost recovered, but now Ireland
is on the brink of civil war. There are
divided loyalties in Katie's family – how
can Katie make a choice? Who is right?

Paperback €6.95/STG£4.99

THE CINNAMON TREE

When she steps on a landmine, Yola
Abonda's leg is shattered, and with it her
dreams for the future. Who will want her
now? Yola travels to Ireland for treatment
and makes a special friend – Fintan. She
returns home with a mission: to do all she
can to end the menace of landmines.

Paperback €7.95/STG5.99